"If you want to be illuminated about what happens in the confines of the erotic dancing club, this is certainly the book to read. It is outstanding at challenging the myths circulated in popular culture. Its uniqueness is based on bringing a global perspective on a relational labour economy to a local form of consumption by interweaving the voices of the dancers, managers and owners through a nuanced analysis of why, what and how."

Beverley Skeggs, Professor of Sociology, Goldsmiths,
University of London, UK

"*Flexible Workers* lives up to its promise to consider the voices of exotic dancers in dialogue with wider political, economic, and legal shifts in the UK. Moving beyond micro-sociological analyses of the strip club, Sanders and Hardy present a holistic exploration of the landscape of exotic dance, focusing on the social and economic conditions that produce and enable its consumption. The impact of widespread social changes, exploitative labor markets, and ill-founded regulation is deftly illustrated through interviews with dancers, whose bodies are too often disciplined and controlled in the name of 'protection'."

Katherine Frank, Scholar-in-Residence, American University, USA

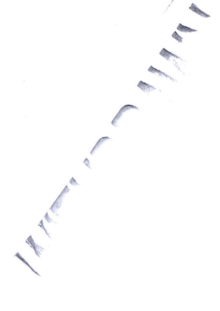

Flexible Workers

Striptease and other types of erotic dance increasingly make up a large, lucrative and visible part of the sex industries in the United Kingdom, and 'lap dancing' has become the focus of many important contemporary debates about gender, work and sexuality. This new book from Teela Sanders and Kate Hardy moves away from the more traditional focus on the relations between dancers and customers to a focus on regulation and the working conditions experienced by individuals in stripping work. Drawing on interviews, survey data and participant observation with dancers, managers, regulators and other staff, Sanders and Hardy present the first ever nationwide study of the stripping industry and the working lives of those within it.

The book explores the reasons for the expansion of the industry in the United Kingdom and the experiences, opinions and perspectives of those who produce and shape it. Placing dancers' voices centre stage, it examines the wider political economy which shapes dancers' engagement in employment in the stripping industry, pointing towards the wider conditions of the labour market and growing privatisation of higher education as explanatory factors for its labour supply. In suggesting a new feminist politics of stripping, dancers voice their own political awareness of erotic dance and an intersectional analysis of solidarity with workers in the stripping industry is foregrounded.

Presenting a 360-degree view of the industry, this groundbreaking study presents systematic evidence for the first time on this area of social life which has become central as a strategy of survival, class mobility and urban accumulation. It will appeal to undergraduate and post-graduate students and researchers across the fields of criminology, sociology, geography, labour studies and gender studies, as well as regulators, activists and even dancers themselves.

Teela Sanders is a Reader in Sociology at the University of Leeds with qualifications in both sociology and social work. Working at the intersections of sociology, criminology and social policy, she has published extensively in areas germane to sexuality/gender and regulation. Monographs to date include: *Sex Work. A Risky Business* (Willan, 2005) and *Paying for Pleasure: Men who Buy Sex* (Willan, 2008). Co-authored texts include *Prostitution: Sex Work, Policy and Practice* (Sage, 2009). She has co-edited *New Sociologies of Sex Work* (Ashgate, 2010), *Body/Sex/Work – Intimate, Embodied and Sexualised Labour* (Palgrave, 2013) and *Social Policies and Social Control: New Perspectives on the Not-so-Big Society* (Policy Press, 2014).

Kate Hardy is a Lecturer in Work and Employment Relations at the Leeds University Business School. Her research explores a feminist political economy of labour, with a particular focus on non-standard forms of work and the intersections between paid and non-paid forms of labour, work, employment and the body. Her research and scholarship is informed by a commitment to social change and a desire to bridge academia and activism through involvement in the feminist movement and other spaces of political activity. She has co-edited *Body/Sex/Work – Intimate, Embodied and Sexualised Labour* (Palgrave, 2013) and *New Sociologies of Sex Work* (Ashgate, 2010) and has articles in a number of journals, including the *British Journal of Sociology, Work, Employment and Society* and *Emotion, Space and Society*.

Routledge Studies in Crime and Society

Flexible Workers

Labour, regulation and the political economy of the stripping industry

Teela Sanders and Kate Hardy

Routledge
Taylor & Francis Group

LONDON AND NEW YORK

First published 2014
by Routledge

2 Park Square, Milton Park, Abingdon, Oxon OX14 4RN
711 Third Avenue, New York, NY 10017, USA

Routledge is an imprint of the Taylor & Francis Group, an informa business

First issued in paperback 2016

British Library Cataloguing in Publication Data
A catalogue record for this book is available from the British Library

Library of Congress Cataloging-in-Publication Data
Sanders, Teela.
    Flexible workers : labour, regulation and the political economy of the stripping industry /
Teela Sanders and Kate Hardy.
    pages cm.—(Routledge studies in crime and society ; 10)
    1. Sex-oriented businesses—Great Britain. 2. Sex-oriented businesses—
Law and legislation—Great Britain. 3. Stripteasers—Great Britain.
    4. Lap dancers—Great Britain. I. Hardy, Kate, 1983– II. Title.
    HQ185.A5S248 2014
    363.40941—dc23
    2013040694

ISBN 978–1–138–66534–7 (pbk)
ISBN 978–0–415–67918–3 (hbk)
ISBN 978–1–315–79803–5 (ebk)

Typeset in Times New Roman
by Swales & Willis Ltd, Exeter, Devon

Contents

List of illustrations

Figures

Tables

Acknowledgements

As with any research project, we incurred great debts both in undertaking the fieldwork for this book and in the writing up process itself. First, we would like to thank the Economic and Social Research Council (ESRC) for the resources to carry out both of the projects reported in this book. Despite resistance against taking issues of 'lap dancing' (and sex work more broadly) seriously as a matter for scholarly inquiry and public funds, we are grateful that the ESRC and the reviewers recognised the academic and political relevance of such a project. We are pleased to have been able to undertake a rigorous, well-resourced project in order to give voice to the thousands of people who work each day in the stripping industry.

The Steering Committee for the 'Regulatory Dance' project helped initiate and shape an ambitious project, so thanks to Maggie O'Neill, Phil Hadfield, Rachela Colosi, Catherine Stephens and Rosie Campbell for their time, input, sage guidance and continued support. We thank Liz Lock for her thoughtful photographic work with the participants, which has enabled the project to move beyond the written word and to generate visual artefacts which counter the perennially reproduced stereotyped images of women and stripping work. We would also like to express our gratitude to Charlie Pycraft for kindly permitting us to include the Hackney Dancers Alliance protest image. Marie Johnson in the School of Sociology and Social Policy, University of Leeds never failed to respond to our tireless administrative demands and Susan Holden at Leeds City Council was a great help in terms of access. Writing is always a collaborative process and we have benefited greatly from the insightful thoughts of a number of people. Laura Jarvis, Katie Cruz, Ron Roberts, Crystal Jackson, Megan Rivers-Moore, Tom Gillespie, Ellis Slack, Laura Schwartz and Jane Hardy all developed the ideas in this book through their theoretical late night reading, reflections and suggestions. We owe them all a great intellectual debt. Kate Brown has been a strong supporter of this project from the beginning, ranging from the analysis she undertook on our interviews and her insightful reflections on the early data. The book would have suffered greatly without this creative and thoughtful input.

Rosie Campbell was pivotal in the impact and dissemination project 'Regulating Working Conditions: Sexual Entertainment Venues' which is reported in Chapter 7. Both projects would not have been possible without the acceptance and involvement of the wider dancer community. We specifically want to thank Laura Newis, Solitaire and Sarah Vernon, and those involved in the outreach for the iphone App, in particular Vera Rodriguez and Suzanna Slack, whose tireless efforts did not go unnoticed. Equally, members of the industry who opened their strip club doors and pushed aside their suspicions to enable the research and dissemination were key to the project. We hope in time they will agree to spend some of their profits on further research into improving standards across the strip club industry.

Most of all, we would like to thank the two hundred dancers who took the time to participate in this project in one form or another. We hope that we have done justice to the stories that you gave us and that we have been able to give voice to your articulate ideas, critiques and theorisations of yourselves, your lives and your work. We hope that this book enables readers to hear your voices and, just maybe, to work with you to make the changes that you want to see in your working lives.

Introduction
Beyond the stripping wars

On 22 November 2008, 2000 women marched through the bitterly cold streets of London to demand an end to violence against women. The route snaked through the West End, past the historic red light district of Soho and on to Tottenham Court Road, passing Spearmint Rhino, one of the biggest strip clubs in London. Upon approaching the club, a group of women broke away from the main march and began to jeer and direct chants at the building, 'I object to objectification, just for sexual gratification', and to sing (to the tune of *Glory Glory Hallelujah*) 'Women's bodies not for sale, Women's bodies not for sale, Women's bodies not for sale, And we won't be for sale no more!' They were soon joined by a second group, vivified by bright red umbrellas, their placards reading 'Sex Workers need Feminists, Feminists need Sex Workers', 'Criminalisation is Violence against Workers' and 'I Support Sex Workers' Rights'. The second group of women formed a block across the front of the building, creating a human shield from the voices of the first. A sound clash emerged, as the bodies with red umbrellas chanted back 'Sex Workers' Rights Are Human Rights', each attempting to drown the other out, until the first group moved on, leaving the second, a visual artefact of their solidarity with the women inside, their message loud and clear in the cold November night.

Striptease and other types of erotic dance increasingly make up a large, lucrative and visible part of the sex industries in the UK, reflecting trends in other developed economies (Deshotels and Forsyth 2005; Penttinen 2010; Scoular and Sanders 2010). It is thought to be one of the fastest-growing sectors of the leisure industry and night-time economy, with a turnover of £300 million (Jones et al. 2003; Edwards 2009). In 1995, the industry most clearly entered the world of global corporate capital when Rick's Cabaret International Inc. became the first club traded on the NASDAQ (the second largest stock market in the world, after the New York Stock Exchange).

The expansion and formal subsumption of this particular sector of the sex industry, as it has been fully incorporated in mainstream circuits of capital, has led to fierce debates amongst feminist activists, academics and local and national policy makers. In the mid-2000s, some sections of the public became concerned with what they saw as the proliferation or 'growing tide' of 'lap dancing' across the country (Bindel 2004; Object 2008). Campaigners argued for measures which would stem this expansion and ultimately shut down places in which striptease occurred. The issue of 'lap dancing' clubs became a flashpoint, dividing the feminist movement in often violent and aggressive ways. The sound clash of the two feminist groups on the Reclaim the Night march described above acts as a metaphor for the way in which debates around the stripping industry have developed in scholarship, activism, the media, and government policy in the UK. Amidst the political heat that this generated, the issue of striptease rose up the political agenda, as much in feminist activism as in local planning and national-scale legislative debates.

In the midst of these debates, little systematic evidence existed about the conditions in which women worked. Critiques of the industry tended to exist on a moral register, focusing on its 'effects' on people walking past and the local area (Hubbard and Colosi 2013), with little reference to the actual conditions of work, or women's experiences inside the clubs. To address this vacuum, the research on which this book is based sought to examine why and how there had been a rise and integration of sexual entertainment in the night-time economy. Importantly, it places the voices of dancers centre stage, privileging the everyday lived experiences of workers in the stripping industry. Yet we strive to do more. We try to consider the voices of the dancers in 'conversation' with wider political–economic shifts, as well as how these shifts are played out through employer practices and relations with workers.

The timing of this investigation was particularly pertinent, occurring at a time when the legislation on licensing stripping was undergoing an overhaul and a new national regime of regulation was introduced (see Chapter 3). The study was also undertaken in the context of the immediate aftermath of the economic crisis of 2008 and the ongoing recession and austerity measures put into place by the Conservative–Liberal Democrat Coalition government, not least, but including, the trebling of tuition fees for undergraduate study. The effect on workplaces and the labour market has been marked, with managers reporting wage cuts or freezes, preventing new vacancies and postponing plans to expand workforces, as well as the doubling of 'zero hours' contracts (van Wanrooy et al. 2011). In combination with dramatic cuts in public sector employment, traditionally a female domain, all these conditions resulted in a hostile and difficult labour market, particularly for young people, with unemployment rates amongst 16 to 24 year olds at 20 per cent in 2010 (Taylor and Gush 2012).

The term 'lap dancing' has become synonymous with all forms of erotic dance or striptease in the UK. Yet while labour processes, styles of dance and organisational structures of work differ across a spectrum of venues, 'lap dancing' is in fact not licensed in the UK and does not exist as a legal category. As a result, throughout this book we refer to women who dance to music and remove their clothes as 'dancers' or 'performers' and to the broader labour process as 'stripping work'. In what follows we discuss the variation between these venues and the labour they require, hoping to emphasise and do justice to the ambivalences and uneven geographies within the landscape of striptease in the UK. We conceptualise strip-ping work as *work*, as part of the 'sex industries', as well as part of a broader continuum in which women's labour is sexualised, irrespective of industry. Due to its heterogenous nature, it is always prudent to discuss the sex industries in the plural in order to capture the varying social and economic relations, labour proc-esses, structures of domination and exploitation, spaces and times in which sexual labour is sold.

'The growing tide' of 'lap dancing'

In the mid-2000s, concerns began to grow around the apparent expansion of the striptease industry and its changing geography, which saw it shift from the social and spatial margins to urban centres. Fears and distaste for this 'proliferation' or 'growing tide' (Object 2008: 4) led to demands by campaigners to control the 'rapid expansion' of striptease venues across the country. Using blunt calculations which enumerated licensing applications refused (2) and approved (10) over a six-month period in 2008, the campaign group Object began to call for legislative change to stem the so-called growing tide. Such metrication cannot account for the fluid and fast-changing nature of the industry and its high turnover of owners, licenses and venues. Applications granted do not automatically convert into the opening of a new club, and clubs frequently close down after a few months due to saturation of the market. While it is hard to refute the claim that there has been an increase in the *number* of clubs over the last ten years, it is important to note that this does not equate to an equivalent increase in consumption (or 'demand'). Further, the affective sense that striptease has become more mainstreamed may relate more to its spatial shift to town centres and the gentrification of tradition-ally working-class areas, leading to higher levels of middle-class exposure to strip venues, than to purely quantitative increases. As we argue, the apparent visible expansion of clubs (a growing number of venues) does not necessarily reflect a rise in custom, as many venues can be kept afloat with minimal demand due to the structure of value appropriation, which is primarily premised on house fees paid by dancers, irrespective of the level of consumption. Despite these meth-odological flaws in metrication, such a partial counting exercise was used as part of a powerful campaign to convince residents and local politicians that the strip industry was spiralling out of control in order to discursively produce the image of a 'social problem' requiring intervention, particularly in the form of licensing regulations (with the ultimate aim of shrinking of the industry).

Methodology

Funded by the Economic and Social Research Council (RES-000–22–3163), this book is a result of a large-scale, multi-method project exploring the rise of the strip-based entertainment industry in the UK and the experiences and conditions of those who work in it. Carried out in England and Wales during 2010 to 2013, 'The Regulatory Dance' is the largest study to date of the strip-based entertainment

In our project, using a photographer with experience of working with people in the sex industries, dancers were asked to guide the photographer in shots that they felt were important to them. The photographs of their workplace, their work routines and their activities 'at work' were used to convey meaning about dancers' perspectives on their working lives, which could be communicated to a broader audience. This sought to dislodge the gaze on women's bodies, particularly the imagery of high-heeled shoes hooked on a stool or of dancers' bare backs, to produce a perspective from the positionality of dancers' own gaze. The photographer, Liz Lock, worked with three dancers who choreographed a set of images which represented their work, workplace and work routines. The pictures that emerged focused on the materiality of work: sandwiches in a sports bag for the dancers' dinner; the harsh white lights of the changing room; or the signing in book, a source of disciplinary power over workers.[2]

As researchers who have long-standing links with sex workers, who consider themselves 'allies' of sex workers' movements and who have over a decade of experience researching the sex industry, our experiences did not resonate with those of Wesley's (2006), who felt at times her identity and physical safety were at risk during strip club research. We do, however, connect with her experience that the privileges of the academic status and protections this affords enables us more control and choice over our actions than perhaps that of some of the women who took part in the research, not in least due to permanent salaried contracts. Further, we recognise the ways in which our research, although grounded in conditions of alliance with workers in the sex industry, also depends on their participation for our jobs and careers. We hope that, in some way, our desire to create space for dancers' voices, inclusion of dancers in the research process and the ways in which our research has been mobilised in attempting to improve working conditions for dancers (Chapter 7), goes some way in mediating the risk that we make careers on the 'backs' of sex workers (Metzenrath 1998: no page).

It is important to note here that customers were not part of our empirical project, though of course they were discussed with interviewees as part of conversations relating to the organisation and interactions in the club. There is, however, detailed and extensive research which explores the interactions between dancers and customers, customers understanding of their engagement in strip clubs in relation to their everyday lives, motivations for visiting and their own 'performances of desire' (Frank 1998). The idea that men visit for sexual release only has been challenged and instead it has been suggested that motivations are also driven by a range of other masculine-affirming qualities such as enjoying safe but exciting leisure, sexualised interactions with women without the pressure of their own physical performance, and their own narratives of monogamy and commitment to marriage (Frank 2002, 2003; Egan 2003, 2006). Typologies have been developed to describe the different 'types' of customers (Erickson and Tewsbury 2000) and particular emphasis has been placed on the distinction between 'regulars' and more casual customers (Egan 2003, 2006; Brewster 2003). While it was not within our remit to explore this, due to our focus on the strip club as workplace, important questions remain about the desire to consume sexual labour and the social and economic conditions which produce and enable its consumption.

Key arguments

This book specifically adds to the 'polymorphous paradigm' of sex-work research, which emphasises a varied 'constellation of occupational arrangements, power relations, and worker experiences' within paid sexual services and performances (Weitzer 2010: 26). Framing the research in this paradigm achieves these ends by offering a complex picture of the structure, nature and working population of the stripping industry in the UK at a particular moment in time characterised by change, challenge and economic downturn. Responding to Weitzer's call to utilise the polymorphous paradigm, and that of Agustin's (2005) call to locate sex work and sex workers in their cultural context, we hope to contest commonplace mythologies about stripping work and inform public policy in order to bring about direct change to improve the working conditions of dancers. Beyond this public sociology or action-orientated focus, however, we also contribute to theoretical understandings in a range of ways that enable further understanding of the stripping industry and sexual labour and consumption.

First, we contest the idea of proliferation or a 'growing tide' of stripping solely attributed to a rise in misogyny or a culture of 'objectification', demonstrating instead that the growth was attached to the boom economy of the 2000s and the cultures of consumption that accompanied it, as well as the micro-economics of clubs which developed multiple methods for extracting surplus value from workers, while shifting all risk onto their shoulders. In relation to this, we argue that the consumption of stripping appears to have peaked and may now be in decline, due to a variety of mediating and interwoven cultural, legal, social and economic dynamics.

Second, we demonstrate how the continuous supply of labour (rather than demand) explains the reasons for the expansion of this industry during the 1990s to 2010s and its relative buoyancy during the recession. We explore how the 'disposability of labour' and the wider political economy of reductions in real wages, the privatisation of higher education and the limited availability of sufficiently paid part-time work underpins the resilience of the industry and its ability to extract value and profit.

Third, we argue that regulation of the striptease industry has taken the form of 'empty shell' licensing, in which some elements of erotic dance are highly regulated, while the exploitation of dancers and regulation of their working conditions remains outside legal frameworks. However, we demonstrate – with examples of good practice – that this does not need to be the case. We present evidence from a follow-on impact and dissemination project which has made a direct impact on licensing policy, and – we hope – the working conditions experienced by some dancers.

In addition to these key theoretical contributions, we offer an understanding of the wider political economy in which the strip industry is regulated, including an overview of the discourses that led to the reform in licensing and the introduction of Sexual Entertainment Venue policies. Addressing issues relating to the labour of stripping, we emphasise the multiple forms of labour involved in stripping work and we suggest these are relationally produced in the interaction between the dancer and the customer in what we have termed an 'attention economy'. We also align the labour conditions found in the strip industry with other contemporary developments in labour relations.

Finally, in emphasising the voices of dancers throughout the book, we demonstrate dancers' political awareness of the politics surrounding erotic dance and illustrate that they actively reject the dominant feminist narrative, constructing their own – often feminist – analyses of the politics of their work. Organising is embryonic amongst dancers and we point to examples of local activism that have sought to influence the politics of erotic dance, protect their livelihoods and change their conditions of work.

Structure

This book responds to a series of research questions about the stripping industry, including why it appears to have expanded in such a way as to appear frequently in the high streets of towns and cities across the UK, who the women are that work in the industry and which wider socio-economic trends are shaping these processes.

In Chapter 1, we first discuss the rise of stripping as a site of labour, leisure and consumption in the UK, exploring the interconnecting ways in which strip-based entertainment has been mainstreamed. Presenting a detailed overview of the contemporary landscape of the strip industry, we briefly look at the history of stripping in the UK before describing the contemporary form that this labour takes and mapping out its organisation through agencies, pub and club management.

Chapter 2 discusses the narratives that have shaped the debates on exotic dance, sketching out the discursive landscape that has moved from the pathologisation of dancers to the recognition of dancing as labour practice. Setting out the radical feminist position on the one hand and 'feminist politics of stripping' on the other, we discuss the range of feminist thinking of these issues. Briefly tracing the micro-sociological analyses of stigma, relationships and identity, we note the gaps in relation to exploring labour conditions, processes and work in a systematic way, particularly in the empirical context of the UK. We explore existing theoretical and conceptual approaches to understanding the labour process, employment relations and rules and regulations which govern dancers' labour. Since much of this literature is drawn from North America and from the United States in particular, in the last part of this chapter we outline existing knowledge about dancing drawn from recent literature based in the UK, highlighting where our contributions fit.

In Chapter 3 we map out the changing legal terrain in the licensing of striptease from 2008 to 2012 in the UK. We trace the narratives that informed the reform process which centre on 'resident's power'; assumptions and concerns about crime and anti-social behaviour; and radical feminist discourses which contest the activity on ideological and moral terms. In the midst of these dominant voices and narratives, we describe how dancers' voices and narratives are hard to locate. This chapter outlines the legal reforms that took place and the current framework of Sexual Entertainment Venue policy which governs striptease venues, as well as how local authorities have responded and the consequences of the new legislation in relation to dancers working conditions. The chapter argues that the licensing reforms have produced an 'empty shell' in which dancers' working conditions remain almost entirely unregulated.

Chapter 4 focuses on the multiple ways in which value and profit is extracted from dancers in clubs in the form of house fees, commission, fines and tips. In addition to describing the apparently contradictory nature of dancers' 'self-employment' in the club due to the mechanisms of control and discipline they face, we also depict the physical conditions, including health and safety issues, dancers experience in the workplace. The conditions of the workplace – in particular the high house fees, growing numbers of dancers and decreased demand – we argue, encourage a 'race to the bottom' whereby some dancers undercut others, leading to work intensification in the form of 'extras'.

Many aspersions are cast about women who work as strippers, alluding to their reasons for working in the industry and the ways in which they made the decision to do so. In order to provide empirical evidence from which to confirm or refute these claims, in Chapter 5 we draw on survey and interview data to explore the demographic of women working in the industry and the reasons they offer for working in it. We develop a typology of dancers, divided into 'Professionals' 'Pragmatists' and 'Strategists', who each use dancing differently, fitting it alongside other life strategies and activities. The overarching claim is that, in most cases, dancing is used strategically, generally as a short-term tactic to enable longer-term future-orientated goals outside the sex industry.

In Chapter 6 we explore the nature of stripping as a form a labour. Although this has been widely explored elsewhere (we outline these arguments in some depth in Chapter 2), in this chapter we take a novel approach in examining dancers' labour in the chronological format that it is performed. We demonstrate the multifarious skills and forms of labour that are drawn upon. Drawing on previous research, we make the novel argument that not only is this 'relational labour', but also that the very type of labour that is consumed is produced relationally, emerging from a negotiation between the desires of the customer and the labour that the dancer is willing to perform. We theorise this as an 'attention economy' and argue that it is attention and recognition that are the key products purchased in the stripping encounter, particularly during the private dance.

The relationship between management and licensing is examined in Chapter 7, an unexplored terrain in the context of the UK. This chapter uses detailed empirical evidence to map the levels of compliance by clubs and general issues faced by licensing officials with regards to the operations of strip clubs. We argue that dancers fall between the gaps in terms of the responsibility of different government agencies and we illustrate that the dancer *qua* worker has been invisible in licensing, appearing only in terms of a nude body and individualised body parts.

Other concerns around managing risk, community concerns and perceptions take precedence over workers rights and well-being in the current licensing framework. Despite this, we illustrate a point of optimism due to local authorities' powers to include working conditions within licensing conditions since 2010. We describe how it is at this meso-level where there is the possibility of leverage for change. Examples are given from an impact study which emerged from the research, which worked directly with local authorities to influence and change Sexual Entertainment Venue policies, in order to show how these local partnerships can make changes to everyday working conditions. Although dancers' interests were not written into the reform, an unintended consequence has been the creation of space within the regulatory framework to shape the industry in favour of dancers working conditions.

In Chapter 8 we turn the focus back to the 'politics of stripping', conceptualising it in its widest form. We examine the ways in which, although their voices are frequently silenced, dancers 'speak back'. In placing their voices side by side with those that claim to speak on their behalf, we demonstrate that dancers' are highly conscious of the claims made in their name and frequently and articulately refute them, even expressing anger and disbelief about the ways in which they are represented. Beyond negation of the ways in which others claim to act on their behalf, we also outline the ways in which dancers themselves would seek to improve their industry. Dancers were highly critical of the ways in which the industry was managed, instead offering suggestions of the ways in which the industry could improve. Finally, we consider collective organisation amongst the dancers as a key mechanism for changing working conditions inside striptease venues. We first examine the case of the London boroughs of Hackney and Tower Hamlets, in which 'nil policies' were recommended by the council, spurring localised action and, second, the possibilities for collective organisation in more traditional organisations such as unions and other self-organised social movements.

Overall, we offer the first nationwide study on erotic dance ever undertaken in the UK. While we cannot speak on behalf of all or even any dancers, what we present here is an image of the landscape of erotic dance, examining the working conditions, regulation and changes in the industry, as well as suggesting the ways in which it may be improved in the future. Moving beyond micro-sociologies of the strip club, we move between the scales at which it is constituted, from the relations between the dancers and customers and the labour produced, the organisational structures that shape and gain value from that labour and the wider political landscape in which the place of 'lap dancing' is contested. Throughout these discussions we weave in the very voices which have so often disappeared in most public debates over the industry: the women themselves who strip for a living.

Notes

1 This included: Aberdeen, Aldershot, Aylesbury, Birmingham, Blackpool, Boston, Bournemouth, Brighton, Chatham, Croydon, Doncaster, Edinburgh, Glasgow, Grantham, Harrogate, Hayes, Huddersfield, Hull, Kent, Leeds, Leicester, Lincoln, Liverpool, London, Maidenhead, Manchester, Milton Keynes, Newcastle, Nottingham, Peterborough,

Plymouth, Portsmouth, Scarborough, Sheffield, Skegness, Stratford, Sunderland, Tamworth, Twickenham, Uxbridge, Wakefield, Watford and York. Dancers also discussed their experiences outside the UK in places such as Canada, Greece, Denmark, Italy, Australia, Romania, Portugal, Malta, Spain, Ibiza, Belgium, the United States, Caribbean and Austria.

2 The photographic film can be found at www.youtube.com/watch?v=MPqIhWD8UQk.

References

Agustin, L.M. (2005) New research directions: the cultural studies of commercial sex, *Sexualities* 8 (5): 618–31.

Bindel, J. (2004) *Possible Exploits: Lap Dancing in the UK*, Glasgow: Glasgow City Council.

Brewster Z.W. (2003) Behavioural and interactional patrons: tipping techniques and club attendance, *Deviant Behaviour: An Interdisciplinary Journal* 24 (2): 221–43.

Cheng, S. (2013) Private lives of public women: photos of sex workers (minus the sex) in South Korea, *Sexualities* 16 (1–2): 30–42.

Deshotels, T. and Forsyth, C. (2005) Strategic flirting and the emotional tab of exotic dancing, *Deviant Behavior* 21 (2): 223–41.

Edwards, C. (2009) *A Controlled Dance: Lap Dancing and the Question of its Regulation*, undergraduate criminology dissertation, University of Leeds.

Egan, D. (2003) 'I'll be your fantasy girl, if you'll be my money man': mapping desire, fantasy and power in two exotic dance clubs, *Journal of Psychoanalysis, Culture and Society* 8 (1): 109–20.

Egan, D. (2006) *Dancing for Dollars and Paying for Love: The Relationships Between Exotic Dancers and Their Regular*, Basingstoke: Palgrave Macmillan.

Erickson, J. and Tewksbury, X. (2000) The 'gentlemen' in the Club: a typology of strip club patrons, *Deviant Behaviour: An Interdisciplinary Journal* 21 (2): 271–93.

Frank, K. (1998) The production of identity and the negotiation of intimacy in a gentleman's club, *Sexualities* 1 (2): 175–201.

Frank, K. (2002) *G-Strings and Sympathy: Strip Club Regulars and Male Desire*, London: Duke University Press.

Frank, K. (2003) 'Just trying to relax': masculinity, masculizing practices and strip club regulars, *Journal of Sex Research* 40 (1): 61–76.

Hubbard, P. and Colosi, R. (2013) Sex, crime and the city: municipal law and the regulation of sexual entertainment, *Social and Legal Studies* 22 (1): 67–86.

Jones, P., Shears, P. and Hillier, D. (2003) Retailing and the regulatory state: a case study of lapdancing clubs in the UK, *International Journal of Retail and Distribution Management* 31 (4): 214–19.

Liepe-Levinson, K. (2002) *Strip Show: Performances of Gender and Desire*, New York: Routledge.

Mai, N. (2009) *Final Policy Relevant Document: ESRC Project Migrant Workers in the UK Sex Industry*. Online: https://metranet.londonmet.ac.uk/research-units/iset/projects/esrc-migrant-workers.cfm.

Metzenrath, S. (1998) In touch with the needs of sex workers, *Research For Sex Work 1*. Online: http://plone.nswp.org/nswp-in-action/r4sw/research-for-sex- work-1.

Object (2008) Stripping the illusion: countering lap dancing industry claims. Online: www.object.org.uk/index.php?option=com_content&view=article&id=1&Itemid=11 (accessed 10 July 2013).

O'Neill, M. (2010) Cultural criminology and sex work: resisting regulation through radical democracy and Participatory Action Research (PAR), *Journal of Law and Society* 37 (1): 210–32.

Penttinen, E. (2010) Imagined and embodied spaces in the global sex industry, *Gender, Work and Organization* 17 (1): 28–44.

Pilcher, K. (2012) Performing in a night-time leisure venue: a visual analysis of erotic dance, *Sociological Research Online* 17 (2). Online: www.socresonline.org.uk/17/2/19. html.

Scoular, J. and Sanders, T. (2010) Introduction: the changing social and legal context of sexual commerce: why regulation matters, *Journal of Law and Society* (Special issue) 37 (1): 1–18.

Taylor, M. and Gush, K. (2012) *Young People and Unemployment: The Double Penalty*. ISER, University of Essex. Online: www.iser.essex.ac.uk/publications/iser-reports/2011–12/young-people-and-unemployment-the-double-penalty (accessed 27 September 2013).

Van de Meulen, E. (2011) Action Research with sex workers: dismantling barriers and building bridges, *Action Research* 9 (4): 370–84.

Van Wanrooy, B., Bewley, H., Bryson, A., Forth, J., Freeth, S., Stokes, L. and Wood, S. (2011) *Workplace Employment Relations Study: First Findings*. Online: www.gov.uk.

Weitzer, R. (2010) The mythology of prostitution: advocacy research and public policy, *Sex Research and Social Policy* 7 (1): 15–29.

Wesely, J. (2006) Negotiating myself: the impact of studying female exotic dancers on a feminist researcher, *Qualitative Inquiry* 12 (1): 146–62.

1 Locating the strip-based entertainment industry

Introduction

This chapter sets the scene of the strip-based industry in the UK at the beginning of the twenty-first century. We start by contextualising the industry within the broader sociological changes of the night-time economy expansion and the economic and cultural mainstreaming of the sex industry on a macro and global level as well as at a local level. It is in this initial section that we problematise whether strip work is actually part of the sex industries, arguing that it does constitute part of the sex industries in that what is commodified in this exchange is a particularly sexualised service and labour process. Second, we sketch out the historical landscapes that provide the backdrop for the development of the industry and demonstrate the ways in which it has changed, particularly in relation to new regimes of licensing and regulation. Third, we map out the previous and current characteristics and organisation of the industry, in particular the business models of strip venues in the UK. Finally, we outline dancers' labour process and the product that is produced, exchanged and consumed in these contexts before returning to it in more depth in following chapters (see Chapter 6).

Mainstreaming striptease

The boom from the mid-1990s to 2008 particularly centred on the geographic space of the City of London with the circulation of capital there and its wider financial markets laying the foundations for the growth of the modern-day 'lap dancing' industry.[1] 'Corporate masculinity' (Allison 1994), in which 'a particular masculinized set of performances is more highly valorized than other ways of being in the workplace' (McDowell 2010: 653) is certainly accountable for many of the practices in the consumption of lap dancing: conspicuous consumption in terms of the purchase of unnecessary and overpriced drinks, cultures of excess, high disposable incomes and corporate credit cards. Kynaston (2001: 791) has pointed to the 'City cultural supremacy' in the ways in which the values and practices of the City have reshaped other areas of social life, most obvious, but not limited to, the use of metrics, league tables and emphasis on short-term performance across the business world and also in the NHS and education (Lancaster 2010). Indeed the strip industry markets itself specifically to a city – or simply corporate – male audiences: 'Want to impress your clients? Show them our latest figures' (website marketing from large strip club in northern England). Not limited to practices of business but also to cultural consumption, the cultures of excess that the City has produced led to cultural mimesis, as people visiting high street nightlife sought to mimic the consumption patterns of the elite (Hadfield 2009), leading to the growth of stripping from the capital centre across other towns and cities.

This expansion from the capital to the regions engendered a further spatial shift, with permanent venues offering erotic dance moving from a position on the social and geographical peripheries to a more central position in high streets, town and cities and cultural imaginaries and practices. Sexual desire has always been a motivator to enter city night-time spaces (Arnold 2010), yet the spatial segregation of sites of sexual consumption has always been a key method of policy enforcement activities in attempts to 'cleanse the streets' and move sexual commerce out of view of everyday life (Hubbard 2002; Hubbard and Sanders 2003; Coulmont and Hubbard 2010).

The spatial ordering of the strip industry since the 2003 Licensing Act has been important in generating perceptions of a 'growing tide' of strip venues. These changes were in part 'felt' perceptions, as venues appeared increasingly in city centres and spaces of middle-class consumption, rather than their historic working-class spatialities. This felt perception was therefore due to the increased *visibility* of strip club venues rather than necessarily a highly significant *quantitative* increase. The ways in which this shift from the margins to the mainstream has occurred are explicable in terms of a number of interlocking economic, legal, cultural and social processes, including the rise of the City culture; the expansion of the night-time economy; regulatory changes; the increased visibility of erotic dance in media, fashion and advertising; and changes in the nature of work and employment in the UK.

Over the past two decades, the industry has become increasingly visible and accessible to a wider audience as it has increasingly gained ground as a regular feature of the broader night-time economy (hereafter, NTE) within urban spaces of night-time consumption, diversifying from an elite practice to a frequent feature of popular culture and social rituals, not least including 'stag dos'. Marketing to a more upmarket paying customer with disposable income for such luxuries, Colosi (2010: 23) notes how the range of independently owned, chain and franchised venues have branded themselves as a lifestyle choice for the young professionals, service and finance sector employees. The marketing of the strip venue has moved away from overt signs of sexualisation (in part because of licensing requirements), to merge with the shop fronts and bars of the ordinary NTE. Venues seek to appear more 'luxurious' than the usual pub next door, with a potentially safer environment through visibly increased security and door personnel.

Economically, the rise of the NTE in post-war Britain provided the landscape for urban 'renewal' and a change in the focus and purpose of the cities, as leisure and consumption became significant in the infrastructure of how the city was designed, regenerated and promoted in the move from an industrial to a post-industrial era (Hobbs et al. 2000). The city moved from being an industrial hub, where manufacturing dominated, to an economy where the service and leisure sectors became the main forms of employment and activity (Chatterton and Hollands 2003). The NTE came to be seen as a key player in facilitating urban growth and prosperity, as it emerged as a powerful manifestation of post-industrialism (Hobbs et al. 2000). In this context, the sex industries also found an enabling space for integration into the urban economy (Hubbard et al. 2008).

Instead of ghettoisation in backstreets, away from main leisure zones, erotic dance venues now nestle side by side with ordinary pubs, bars, restaurants and late night venues. As deprived residential and business districts of the city were swept aside to be replaced by multi-national consumer businesses based in state-of-the-art luxury shopping centres and leisure complexes (see examples from Liverpool and Manchester) alongside diversified daytime and night-time leisure spots (such as Manchester's gay village/Canal Street – see Binnie and Skeggs, 2004), which beckon the leisured classes to take part in hedonistic pleasures, so too were spaces made for discreet sex businesses and activities. This integration into the general NTE did not happen by chance, but was enabled and facilitated by broader economic principles and processes. Responding to other marketing processes of 'niche' and increasingly specialised goods and services, striptease has sought to diversify and expand into new untapped markets, particularly focused around changing gendered consumption to cater for women and non-heterosexual customers (Wosick-Correa and Joseph 2008; Pilcher 2011). The strip industry is a diverse one, and whilst the main corporate businesses are aimed at men, and have a female-only dancer workforce, there is increasing variety evident to attend and entice all tastes, preferences and pockets.

This economic mainstreaming has been facilitated by policies encouraging free market economics, entrepreneurship and a premium on individual choice rather than state control, censorship and centralised regulation (Brents and Sanders 2010). While authorities have grappled with achieving a balance between the demand for sexual entertainment with the concerns of communities, property prices, public safety and crime (Hubbard et al. 2009), there have been few legal barriers to the embedding of the industry in urban economies. Geographies of erotic dance therefore contrast with these other spaces of sexual labour and consumption and it is mainly more traditional and direct forms of sex work, such as street prostitution, that has borne the brunt of prohibition and criminalisation (see Sanders 2012 for a review), whilst legal industries have, in contrast, gained visibility and centrality, achieving a real subsumption of women's sexual labour. Emulation of the practices of more 'legitimate' businesses in terms of corporate investment, management protocols and procedures, advertising, marketing and distribution and the 'upscaling' or corporatisation of image and aesthetic have furthered the establishment of erotic dance venues as mainstream.

Cultural factors have also facilitated this visibility and expansion, as the commercialisation of the erotic has taken place through key institutions such as media, television, advertising, fashion, retail and beauty industries. Fensterstock (2006) explains how 'stripper chic' is embroiled in (American) popular culture, from daytime TV, reality shows, high street fashion, music industry production and

Similarly fierce is the distancing of dancers themselves from sex work. The majority of dancers we spoke with did not identify as 'sex workers', but spoke specifically of their dancing status and professional differences with those who may be involved in direct sexual services, such as prostitution or escorting. Such 'othering' and disassociation from sex work is key to the construction of dancer identity and the maintenance of the 'stripper self'.

An examination of the substance of stripping clearly identifies the sexualised nature of the work, the end product being a partially or fully naked dance which is surrounded by sexualised talk and interactions (see Chapter 6). Given the content of the sexual labour, this has led some commentators to note that even though the touch and stripping is sexual, this lends itself to being a 'sexy industry' rather than part of the sex industries, as stripping is a form of adult entertainment (Colosi 2012). Others have looked beyond the sex industries to other activities that promote certain sexualised images and erotic fantasies for consumption: Brooks (2010) calls erotic dance part of the 'desire industries', which includes media, fashion, modelling, acting and selling retail, as they all promote a certain form of image and sexuality. Drawing on the typologies that Harcourt and Donovan (2005) suggest regarding the vast range of sex markets, and the spectrum from direct contact to indirect contact (such as webcam and telephone sex work), it would seem that the labour characteristics, along with the marginal and stigmatised nature of stripping despite its legal status in the UK, definitively place stripping within a broader range of sex markets, as well as in the mainstream industries of the NTE. Yet equally, listening to the majority voice amongst dancers we spoke with, observed and interviewed, their desire to be recognised outside the 'sex worker' status is equally as important, as it sharply identifies how stripping is not about selling sex but a multiple forms of emotional labour.

What does the UK strip industry look like?

Twentieth- and twenty-first-century history

The industry of erotic dance, also known as stripping, striptease, table, pole, or the more Americanised (and sexualised) term 'lap dancing', is one part of the indirect sexual services industry that has grown in the UK over the past twenty years, becoming an integrated and visible aspect of the leisure and night-time economy. This is not a new industry, but one which has merely adapted and changed its nature and presentation (Jarrett 1997). Nude stripping came to London around 1932 at the Windmill Theatre, Soho, London. It can be potentially traced back to Paris in 1875 where public shows consisted of an artist's model undressed to the state of nudity, further developed by the burlesque stripping acts of Gypsy Rose Lee in New York City during the 1930s (Martland 2008). Occupying liminal legal space due to the laws on naked entertainment, differing forms of burlesque and striptease have been part of London's Soho district since at least the 1930s as performers found tricks and skills to circumvent the prohibition of stripping to nude, such as using feathers to hide their genitalia.

Burlesque and striptease (avoiding fully nude) were the main forms of stripping until 1957 when Raymond's Revuebar found a loophole in the law that meant opening as a private members' club would enable full female nudity (see Mort 2006: 29 for an extensive historical overview of stripping in London). Raymond's, which since became an established institution of sexual entertainment, was the first modern-style strip venue in London and was heralded by pleasure seekers as the dawn of a new form of titillating adult entertainment. Later, during the 1970s, stripping pubs also became popular in London.[3] In contrast to clubs such as Raymond's, in these venues dancers were paid by the pub to perform a longer striptease for 15 minutes before full nudity. Increasingly as pubs paid the dancers less money, the 'jug' system developed and eventually took precedence. In this system, dancers solicit each member of the audience for a small payment (usually £1 as a minimum), which is placed in a jug or pint glass before the dance begins. This type of pub remains popular today in specific areas of east and north London, namely in the boroughs of Shoreditch, Hackney and Clerkenwell.

During the 1960s/1970s there was also a notable, if not smaller, strip scene circuit in key urban centres or particular tourist locations such as Torquay, Blackpool, Liverpool, Edinburgh and Manchester. These more established circuits were supported by a steady provision of sports events, hosted by male members' clubs which featured rugby, football, cricket and hockey with stripping as featured entertainment. Alternatively, these venues would be the location of 'stag nights' with strippers performing stage shows to male-only audiences. Alongside this male-orientated presentation of striptease, from the 1970s onwards female strip-o-grams proved to be a popular service brought in to titillate and embarrass the host and audience, performing at private parties (even family events) for short appearances. During this time, there was a limited amount of male striptease available, which developed through national and international troupe touring groups such as the Chippendales, but remains on a small scale even now, appearing either at corporate dance/strip events at theatres or one-off pub 'ladies nights' (see Pilcher 2011; Rambo Ronai and Cross 1998; Smith 2002).

The modern-day product

The most recent change in the strip industry occurred in the mid-1990s when an American import (often known as 'lap dancing') was introduced by the chains Spearmint Rhino and For Your Eyes Only into Greater London (Hubbard 2009). This symbolised the entry of 'lap dancing' into the UK erotic dance market, which gradually began to replace striptease (Hubbard 2009). This type of business offered high street venues where nude dancing could be purchased relatively cheaply, not just in the form of a dancer distantly performing on a stage, but much more intimately through the introduction of the private dance. Research charts the diversification of types of erotic dance, to include lap dancing, striptease and a growing subcultural resurgence of burlesque (Ferreday 2008).

Table 1.1 Services sold by dancers and bought by customers

Type of club	Type of service dancer sells	Approximate cost	Service that customer consumes
Pub	Short stage striptease followed by fully nude stage/pole show (3–5 minutes). No one-to-one interaction other than collecting money, or social chat at the bar.	£1 in pint pot from whole audience.	Nude dancing at a distance, but explicit visuals of dancer's body, athletic stage performance and aesthetic image.
High street licensed strip club	1. One song stage/pole show (not usually to fully nude) every 10–15 minutes (obligatory by management). 2. Private dance – in private booth/space. Striptease to naked, sexualised interactions (though meant to be non-contact). 3. VIP time – private space for one-to-one chat and private dancing 4. Groups – purchase dances from two plus dancers – private dances and stage show to humiliate the stag.	1. Stage show is free as part of the entry fee. 2. £10 for 3 minute dance (£20 in south, £5 in Scotland). 3. £100 per hour. 4. Varies depending on dancers and numbers in group.	1. Semi-naked pole show. 2. Social interaction; emotional labour; sexualised flirting; talk and banter; some touching (possibly caressing) from the dancer in run up to dance. Striptease to naked in intimate proximity and semi-private space (booth or table). 3. Extended period of time of conversation. 4. Private dances, plus staged show which involves more revelry, banter, humour and possibly pranks to humiliate the stag.
High-end gentleman's club	1. Stage shows – semi nude. 2. Private dance – at table/discreet area to naked. 3. VIP – exclusive time with dancer for socialising, dinner, chat and private dances. Mixture of hostessing and stripping.	1. Stage show is free as part of the entry fee. 2. £20 per dancer. 3. £250 per hour.	1. Dancers perform striptease from evening dress to semi-naked. 2. As above. 3. Luxury attention and surroundings for this premium service, sexualised interactions and desire displayed as well as companionship.

Therefore, claims that the industry has proliferated and grown out of control over the past decade are somewhat ahistorical in their claims.

At the time of writing, the website www.ukstripclubs.com has 299 clubs listed for England, 7 for Wales, 20 for Scotland and 0 for Northern Ireland. Yet these raw numbers mask the diverse markets that host striptease. For instance, some of these venues advertise as two separate clubs when in fact they are in the same building (either in the basement or a dedicated VIP room upstairs) and have the same ownership; a few are private parties which are unlicensed events and venues; a few are gay bars (so there is no female stripping), one is a lesbian bar and a small number are hostess bars with private membership and not striptease. London currently offers one licensed strip venue for women (the Candy Bar in Soho), Pilcher (2012) reports on lesbian striptease nights, whilst there has been controversy over gay strip nights in the capital.[4] There is a considerable unlicensed scene organised by dancers, as they organise sporadic private parties in order to seek out entrepreneurial ways to earn more money from stripping and pay less overheads to management. These unlicensed activities are predicted to increase as the new licensing system under the SEV policies allows ordinary venues holding an alcohol or general entertainment licence to host strip nights on an ad hoc basis twelve times a year without a SEV license, therefore avoiding the many licensing conditions adhered to by more formal strip clubs and potentially creating less secure contexts for dancers (see Chapter 3).

Due to the new era of licensing since 2010, whereby the majority of nude entertainment is now licensed through local authority SEV policy, there is now a more accurate quantification of the number of strip clubs. Since the introduction of the legislation there have been 241 strip clubs across the UK issued with SEVs and thirty-one refusals (personal communication with Prof. Phil Hubbard, July 2013). Using these numbers, we can attempt to estimate the size of the workforce in this industry and therefore approximately measure the extent and importance of this type of employment for female workers in the UK. Calculated on the basis that there is an average of sixteen dancers working per night per club in the earlier part of the week (on the basis of 250 clubs), this would mean some 4,000 women dancing in the UK each night. On a Friday and Saturday this could rise to 10,000. Our sources also estimate that these clubs have a labour force of around 20,000 women to call upon in their labour pool. The large clubs in London have 60–100 dancers per night and the largest club chain in London, Secrets, boasts 1,000 female dancers on the books each week to cover its six venues, taken from a pool of approximately 5,000 women who move in and out of the industry to suit their circumstances (personal communication). Such numbers illustrate that erotic dancing is an important employment option for a number of women, a significant proportion of whom are migrant and student women using dancing strategically as an income generator (Sanders 2013). Yet this book is testament that whilst what was considered the 'boom' of the mid-1990s in the majority of the Western world where the strip industry grew (Penttinen 2010), is now on the decline as the industry shrinks across the UK.

Financial crisis and recession

The research for this book took place shortly after the financial crisis of 2008. Whilst there is not sufficient data to substantiate a 'before' and 'after' picture of the industry, accounts from interviewees pay testament to the effects of the recession on the industry. Some managers indicate a 50 per cent fall in profits, whilst dancers refer to a reduction of earning capacity. A reduced number of clients, more difficulties in extracting money from customers and a noted reduction of disposable income all increased the difficulty of making a living in the industry. The erotic dance industry depends on two sources of money: first, disposable income, and second, corporate entertainment accounts. A 2012 report by the Office of National Statistics indicated that disposable income was at a nine-year low across the UK, attesting to the fact that people have less money to spend on luxuries, such as erotic dance (BBC 2012). Unemployment, falls in real wages to the lowest in a decade and inflation on essential items had by 2012 greatly reduced the availability of extra money for consumption of services such as erotic dance. Asked whether the recession was affecting custom, Heidi (26, white British) replied 'Yeah, I think it has. I think it's not a necessity any more, it's more of a luxury. If you're going to cut back on anything it's going to be going to the lap dancing clubs on the side.' Eddie, a manager who was part of a small chain of several clubs, describes how the recession in 2008 was the turning point for closing some of their less profitable clubs located in smaller towns:

> We hit the credit crunch, which wasn't a good thing and we realised there was not much money in places like Smallfield and Townsville, there's not much disposable income in those places. So you're kind of spending the same amount of money on building the place, designing it, you pay the same rent and rates, staff wages, electricity, but you know the money that comes to – so we kind of decided well hang on a minute we'd better kind of get rid of some of the ones that are not making as much money and concentrate on the good ones that we have.
>
> (Eddie, club manager, northern city)

Key to reductions in earning power in London were the removal or reduction of expense accounts, as companies tightened their belts and dictated that corporate entertainment had to be delivered at better value. Dancers certainly noticed the withdrawal of corporate custom from the clubs:

> There used to be loads of [corporate money], hence being able to make loads of money on a weekday years ago, but since the recession, they've cut back luxuries. They got it back on VAT … some clubs have something that will say 'Steak and …' whatever. So that they can get it back on VAT. I used to say sometimes that it comes up as the window cleaners. It stopped because people aren't bringing in … people haven't got the money to do that anymore, to schmooze them.
>
> (Nina, 26, white British)

Bella, an experienced dancer in the city, also recounted how corporate money had dried up:

> Since the recession started, they've [customers] got the money, they just don't want to spend it. Like, taking clients out, the budgets gone down lower. So maybe they used to have £5,000 for taking clients out and showing them a good time or whatever, now they've only got a couple of hundred. So that obviously affects us a lot, because our prices obviously haven't gone down and now it's like 'what, £200 for an half an hour? Oh no. I can't do that'. And because you know you're not going to get that out of them, you end up bargaining.
>
> (Bella, 26, white British)

One partner in a chain of clubs was candid about the impact of the recession and stated that it was possible to make the same amounts of money, but only through work intensification, and also noted that there were regional differences in negative impact:

> Our south coast club and our Midlands club have increased their profitability significantly in the last 18 months. The east coast club has stayed flat, but that's probably the nature of the town. The city club has improved for us but we've had to work much, much harder. You know, we just – you know you've got to give the customers what they want.
>
> (Scott, male owner of chain in the Midlands)

Another owner said that although there was still custom coming through the door, there had been a significant reduction in individual 'big spenders': 'People still spend money. But not as much as they used to. Sometimes you used to get somebody would spend £500, just one person … but you don't get that anymore' (Diane, club owner, northern city). Reductions in income for dancers did not, however, equate to a reduction in income for clubs themselves. Clubs used a strategy of increasing prices for dancers (see also Sanders and Hardy 2012), meaning that lowered levels of custom presented risk only for dancers, rather than club owners. Below, a housemum from a busy London club notes that as dancers had effectively to work twice as many hours for the same money they would earn before the recession, it meant more dancers would come to work more often, thus offering an opportunity to extract more fees and fines:

> They're definitely not earning so much. So in some respects it's better for us because [before] they could come in and do one night and probably earn enough to keep them going, but because – that's better for me, because they have to do two nights … to make up their money.
>
> (Jackie, dance manager, corporate club, southern city)

In this sense, whilst we explain how dancers are earning much less money than before the recession (Chapter 4), profit for larger clubs has not necessarily reduced as dancers are clubs' core means of making money.

The growth of strip clubs is closely associated with the wider expansion of consumption in the UK which ended with the credit crunch and ongoing crisis since 2008. As such, the decline in real wages and therefore disposable income, as well as reductions in corporate spending, have resulted in declining earning opportunities across the industry, with a particularly hard impact on dancers. The apparently high number of clubs that exists project an image of a buoyant industry, despite decreasing demand in terms of quantity of customers and the amounts of money they are willing to spend. In light of this, the cost of keeping clubs open has shifted to dancers through an increase in fees and fines (see Chapter 6), at the same time as the market is flooded with labour, as women find new ways to supplement income or pay for rising costs of living. As such, despite these challenges, the industry across the UK still remains significant as an employer and business sector.

Management and business models in the strip industry

The 'industry' in the UK is demarcated by moderate variation in terms of business models and managerial approaches. Nationally, the industry is made up of different venues and models of organisation, as well as some 'social stratification' (Bradley 2008) in terms of the prices and clientele that clubs seek to attract, although three key models exist, consisting of agencies, pubs and clubs.

Agencies

During the 1970s to 1990s, agencies were a popular mediator between dancers and strippers seeking work and clubs needing performers. Agencies took a fee (from both the dancer and the club) for mediating the relationship for each shift, for special events (such as private parties, sports events and working men's clubs) or on a more permanent basis (Colosi 2010: 3–4). Whilst there is still a presence for stripper agencies placing dancers in venues worldwide, especially in Europe, the UK seems to have largely sidestepped the need for this third-party arrangement. A small number of agencies are still around that supply dancers for one-off events and for related events such as boxing matches and other sports nights.

A minority of dancers had used agencies. Only 7.8 per cent of dancers found their first job through an agency, with this figure dropping to only 3.2 per cent for their second. Some dancers tended to pay agencies a nominal amount (around £10 a month), although, as in clubs, these fees have also been rising since 2008 to around £25 in 2010. It was mainly strip pubs and 'normal' pubs that hosted occasional strip shows that tended to rely on agency labour supply:

> I've just heard with all the other pubs you've got to be with an agency, but here you're not with an agency, you just work there. With agencies, you get sent to all these pubs miles away. When I hear the girls talk about them, it doesn't even seem like it's worth going. Just because they come back with no money.
>
> (Anna, 27 white British)

I found out through a friend of mine about pubs and agencies. There was one major one, and they used to provide dancers to literally all the pubs. The owner used to charge £5 a month for a booking sheet and you could more or less do what you liked, you could more or less choose your bookings and that was it. If you had to travel outside the M25, like to Aldershot or South End, you would get paid an extra £10 or £15 to cover your travel and the clubs used to pay the agency about £10 per girl, per shift. Then, when the other agencies started opening and competing with each other, the way that they managed to undercut each other was not to get the clubs to pay more, but getting the girls to pay their fee.

(Ines, 35, Spanish)

The advantage of agencies was that it was easy to fill a week with shifts and they could guarantee dancers a constant supply of work. Yet agencies often misled dancers, asking them to turn up one to two hours before their time to dance and refusing to offer them support such as maps or full information about the job, venue or audience. Instead, dancers tended to rely on informal knowledge and networks:

You'd need really a friend in the agency to tell you stuff, so I've become good friends with the girl … and I'd phone her up and say 'I've gotta go to the [south London pub] and it says twelve till seven, where is it and do I take my own CDs or is there a jukebox or what's the train station do I go from', all this kind of stuff.

(Faith, 34, white British)

A number of dancers reported agencies sending them to venues that were unsafe, as they tended not to be established venues with facilities and security suitable for erotic dance:

They're … kind of [on the] outskirts of London, kind of little places … where it's just it's really dirty … with no protection and no security and no respect … that's maybe one of the worst sides … but I don't have to put up with now. It's like some of these places … just have no respect for what these girls do and it's – it's so plain is they're just … treated like shit …. you can always make a choice of not going and working there, but often perhaps if you work for an agency you have to do all the venues of the agency.

(Eerikka, 36, Finnish)

At the worst, dancers were asked to change in a cellar and urinate in a bucket. Faith said, however, that despite the poor working conditions, dancers could attract high levels of income, as she 'made four hundred quid and then it didn't seem so bad peeing in a bucket'.

In a classic case of outsourcing, accountability fell into a vacuum, as agencies would blame venues and venues would blame agencies for any problems relating to dancers' welfare, leaving dancers with few avenues for lodging complaints or improving conditions. Agencies that specialised in sending women abroad could

Club management

In clubs, the dominant form of strip venues in the UK, multiple layers of management operated to control the dancers and other aspects of the club. This usually included a general club manager and an assistant club manager, in addition to a 'housemum'. Security/doorstaff were a prerequisite for a licence and played a significant role in operating the security of dancers throughout the shift. Although not specifically considered management, doorstaff were often responsible for both managing the entry of customers and 'marking' dancers (counting how many dances they did) to ensure that the correct rates were paid back to the club by the dancers. This offers a sharp contrast to the pub style of strip venue where dancers are responsible for collecting their earnings in cash, and have much less security, if any, either to control their or the customers' behaviour.

Clubs generally operated in the same manner as all night-time alcohol premises, with daily chores to follow when preparing the venue to be open to the public, for stock to be ready and staff in place. One female worker talks about her role:

> My role is the assistant manageress. I get the girls to work; any questions, any problems the girls have, I deal with that. I cash them in, cash them out. I also speak to the customers on the front desk as well, general banter.
>
> (Jodie, assistant club manager)

Although the dancers are self-employed, independent contractors, they were still managed by strict 'Codes of Conduct' and house rules (see Chapter 4) that were designed to control the dancers behaviour whilst in the workplace.

Given the expansion of full-time, permanent clubs, often located in city centres, the nature of recruitment seems to have changed largely as strippers and dancers are freelance and arrange their own work directly with clubs. The main mode of initial recruitment into their first dancing job was primarily through friends (41.1 per cent), followed by the Internet. However, interestingly, this shifted when dancers moved to their second job as word of mouth became the most common form of recruitment (27 per cent), with friends dropping to 23.8 per cent. Networks are extremely important for recruiting women into dancing and also for them to find decent workplaces. This may be attributable to women's fears about stripping workplaces, which may be put at ease by word of mouth or recommendations, suggesting that trust and tacit knowledge are key in understanding women's mobility in the industry. As self-employed contractors, dancers call up or present themselves at individual clubs and book in for shifts. The more 'high end' London clubs require an audition vetted by management and the 'housemum' (see Chapter 7), but more regularly, high street clubs allow a dancer to have a trial shift whereby they undertake a working audition with customers.

Conclusion

This chapter has provided an outline of the historical and contemporary characteristics of the UK strip industry, its development, diversity and current operating practices. Paying particular attention to the way services are available in each sector of the industry, the nuanced landscape of strip-based entertainment is set out showing that there is organisational variance in how venues operate and shows the 'important cultural and organizational transitions' (Bradley 2008: 504) within the industry over the last twenty years. We have contextualised the striptease entertainment industry in the context of the broader sex industries, its role in the mainstreaming of commercial sex more generally and its evolution alongside changing processes of labour and consumption. To add to this contextualisation, the following chapter reviews relevant academic commentary, debate and research on the area of stripping, mainly from a sociological perspective, to set our contribution to the literature against the background of existing knowledge.

Notes

1 Although it should be noted that due to borough licensing conditions no clubs exist within the City of London, which are instead located in the nearby boroughs of Hackney and Tower Hamlets.
2 Celebrities such as Prince Harry, Pamela Anderson, Scarlett Johansson and Rihanna have all been reported as visiting strip clubs and Stringfellows has a website update on which famous celebrities have visited lately.
3 The photographic book *Baby Oil and Ice: Striptease in the East End* edited by Lara Clifton is a testament to the stripping pubs where a strip show on a stage is performed intermittently and all customers are expected to pay a token amount.
4 www.pinknews.co.uk/2012/01/26/council-no-decision-made-on-gay-pubs-strip-night/.

References

Adkins, L. (1995) *Gendered Work: Sexuality, Family and the Labour Market*, Milton Keynes: Open University Press.
Allison, A. (1994) *Nightwork: Sexuality, Pleasure, and Corporate Masculinity in a Tokyo Hostess Club*, Chicago: University of Chicago Press.
Altman, D. (2002) *Global Sex*, Chicago: University of Chicago Press.
Arnold, C. (2010) *City of Sin: London and Its Vices*, London: Simon and Schuster.
Attwood, F. (2006) Sexed up. Theorising the sexualization of culture, *Sexualities* 9 (1): 7–94.
BBC (2012) Disposable income at nine-year low, ONS figures show, *BBC News*. Online: www.bbc.co.uk/news/business-19060716 (accessed 4 August 2013).
Binnie, J. and Skeggs, B. (2004) Cosmopolitan knowledge and the production and consumption of sexualized space: Manchester's gay village, *Sociological Review* 52 (1): 39–61.
Bradley, M. (2008) Selling sex in the new millenium: thinking about changes in adult entertainment and dancers' lives, *Sociology Compass* 2 (2): 503–18.
Bradley, H., Erickson, M., Stephenson, C. and Williams, S. (2000). *Myths at Work*, Cambridge: Polity Press.
Brents, B.G. and Sanders, T. (2010) The mainstreaming of the sex industry: economic inclusion and social ambivalence, *Journal of Law and Society* 37 (1): 40–60.
Castells, M. (2009) *The Rise of the Network Society: Information Age: Economy, Society, and Culture*, Chichester: Wiley-Blackwell.

Chatterton, P. and Hollands, R. (2003) *Urban Nightscapes: Youth Cultures, Pleasure Spaces and Corporate Power*, London: Routledge.

Collins, A. (2004) Sexuality and sexual services in the urban economy and social scape: an overview, *Urban Studies* 41 (9): 1631–41.

Colosi, R. (2012) *Titillating the Heteronormative: Understanding Customer Motivation in a Lap-dancing Club Setting*, British Sociological Association Conference, University of Leeds.

Colosi, R. (2010) *Dirty Dancing. An Ethnography of Lap-Dancing*, Cullompton, Devon: Willan.

Coulmont, B. and Hubbard, P. (2010). Consuming sex: socio-legal shifts in the space and place of sex shops, *Journal of Law and Society* 37 (1): 189–209.

Fensterstock, A. (2006) Stripper chic: a review essay, in D.R. Egan, K. Frank and M. Johnson (eds) *Flesh for Fantasy. Producing and Consuming Exotic Dance*, New York: Thunder Mouth Press.

Ferreday, D. (2008). 'Showing the girl': the new burlesque, *Feminist Theory* 9 (1): 47–65.

Hadfield, P. (2006) *Bar Wars: Contesting the Night in Contemporary British Cities*, Oxford: Oxford University Press.

Hadfield, P. (2009) From threat to promise: nightclub 'security', governance and consumer elites, *British Journal of Criminology* 48 (6): 429–47.

Harcourt, C. and Donovan, B. (2005). The many faces of sex work, *Sexually Transmitted Diseases* 81: 201–6.

Hobbs, D., Lister, S., Hatfield, P. and Hall, S. (2000) Receiving shadows: governance and liminality in the night-time economy, *British Journal of Sociology* 51 (4): 701–17.

Hochschild, A. (1983). *The Managed Heart*, Berkeley, CA: University of California Press.

Holland, S. (2010) *Pole Dancing, Empowerment and Embodiment*, Basingstoke: Palgrave Macmillan.

Hubbard, P. (2002) Maintaining family values? Cleansing the streets of sex advertising, *Area* 34 (4): 353–60.

Hubbard, P. (2009) Opposing striptopia: the embattled spaces of adult entertainment, *Sexualities* 12 (6): 721–45.

Hubbard, P. and Sanders, T. (2003) Making space for sex work: female street prostitution and the production of urban space, *International Journal of Urban and Regional Research* 27 (1): 73–87.

Hubbard, P., Matthews, R. and Scoular, J. (2009) Legal geographies – controlling sexually oriented businesses: law, licensing and the geographies of a controversial land use, *Urban Geography* 30 (2): 185–205.

Hubbard, P., Matthews, R., Scoular, J. and Agustın, L. (2008) Away from prying eyes? The urban geographies of 'adult' entertainment, *Progress in Human Geography*, 32 (3): 363–81.

Jarrett, L. (1997) *Stripping in Time: A History of Erotic Dancing*, London: Pandora.

Jenson, J., Hagen, E. and Reddy, C. (eds) (1988) *Feminization of the Labour Force*, Cambridge: Polity Press.

Jones, P., Shears, P. and Hillier, D. (2003) Retailing and the regulatory state: a case study of lapdancing clubs in the UK, *International Journal of Retail and Distribution Management* 31 (4): 214–19.

Korczynski, M. and Ott, U. (2004) When production and consumption meet: cultural contradictions and the enchanting myth of customer sovereignty, *Journal of Management Studies* 41 (4): 575–99.

Kynaston, D. (2001) *The City of London. Volume 4: A Club No More 1945–2000*, London: Chatto & Windus.

Lancaster, J. (2010) *Whoops: Why Everyone Owes Everyone and No One Can Pay*, London: Penguin Books.

Martland, B. (2008) *In the Beginning was Theresa: A Personal Illustrated Account of the London Strip Pub Scene since 1976*. Online: www.lulu.com/shop/bill-martland/in-the-begining-there-was-theresa/paperback/product-18606235.html;jsessionid=ACBA89B1FF7E2660943C8BB0D04EF25F.

McDowell, L. (2010). Capital cultures revisited: sex, testosterone and the city, *International Journal of Urban and Regional Research* 34 (3): 652–8.

McNair, B. (2002) *Striptease Culture: Sex, Media and the Democratization of Desire*, London: Routledge.

Moffatt, P.G. and Peters, S.A. (2004) pricing personal services: an empirical study of earnings in the UK prostitution industry, *Scottish Journal of Political Economy* 51 (5): 675–90.

Mort, F. (2006) Striptease: the erotic female body and live sexual entertainment in mid-twentieth century London, *Social History* 32 (1): 27–53.

Object (2008) *Stripping the Illusion: Countering Lap Dancing Industry Claims*. Online: www.object.org.uk/index.php?option=com_content&view=article&id=1&Itemid=11 (accessed 10 July 2013).

Passonen, S., Nikunen, K. and Saarenmaa, L. (2007) *Pornification: Sex and Sexuality in Media Culture*, New York: Berg.

Penttinen, E. (2010) Imagined and embodied spaces in the global sex industry, *Gender, Work and Organization* 17 (1): 28–44.

Pilcher, K. (2011) A 'sexy space' for women? Heterosexual women's experiences of a male strip show venue, *Leisure Studies* 30 (2): 217–35.

Pilcher, K. (2012) Performing in a night-time leisure venue: a visual analysis of erotic dance, *Sociological Research Online* 17 (2). Online: www.socresonline.org.uk/17/2/19.html.

Rambo Ronai, C. and Cross, R. (1998) Dancing with identity: narrative resistance strategies of male and female stripteasers, *Deviant Behavior* 19 (2): 99–119.

Ryder, A. (2004) The changing nature of adult entertainment: between the hard rock of going from strength to strength, *Urban Studies* 41 (9): 1659–1686.

Sanders, E. (2010) Situating the female gaze: understanding (sex) tourism practices in Thailand, in K. Hardy, S. Kingston and T. Sanders (eds) *New Sociologies of Sex Work*, Aldershot: Ashgate.

Sanders, T. (2012) Policing the sex industry, in P. Johnson and D. Dalton (eds) *Policing Sex*, London: Routledge.

Sanders, T. (2013) The advantages and attractions of informality: sex industry work amongst migrants and students in the UK, in P. Saitta, J. Shapland and A. Verhage (eds) *Getting Rich or Getting By? The Formal, Informal, and Criminal Economy in a Globalized World*, The Hague: Eleven Press.

Sanders, T. and Hardy, K. (2012) Devalued, deskilled, and diversified: explaining the proliferation of striptease in the UK, *British Journal of Sociology* 63 (3): 513–32.

Smith, C. (2002) Shiny chests and heaving G-strings: a night out with the Chippendales, *Sexualities* 5 (1) 67–89.

Wosick-Correa, K.R. and Joseph, L.J. (2008) Sexy ladies sexing ladies: women as consumers in strip clubs, *Journal of Sex Research* 45 (3): 201–16.

2 From pathology to labour

The discursive landscape of strip clubs, workers and regulation

Introduction

In 1970, it was possible to claim that strippers and exotic dancers had 'rarely been the subjects of systematic social scientific research' (Skipper and McCaghy 1970: 392). Four decades later there has been an effervescence of interest in this area, producing multiple journal articles and books on the topic. While most of these earlier works focused on stripping in the United States, the apparent growth of strip clubs in the night-time economies, high streets and throughout multiple cultural mediums in the UK has been accompanied by an attendant interest on erotic dance from a small quarter of academic researchers. While our research and analysis is innovative in that it offers the first nationwide study of erotic dance in the UK, our understanding and thinking have been critically informed by what has gone before and the extensive body of work which has now been produced on the topic, particularly from ethnographic 'insider texts'.

Beginning with approaches that framed stripping as a 'deviant' activity and ending with authors who have approached exotic dance squarely as work, this chapter reviews existing research on strip clubs, work and regulation and argues that despite the extent of research, there is still room for a more nuanced perspective on labour, the inter-relationships between dancers, managers and regulators, and the politics of stripping. We argue that the literature on dancing still lacks a multi-scalar, holistic approach to understanding the labour performed in strip clubs and that incorporating such understandings of labour process and the labour market are productive for moving beyond relative micro-sociologies of stripping in different cities and countries. As such we argue for the development of a framework that can account for internal organisational structures and disciplines, as well as statutory regulation and wider cultural, social and gender norms, which we then develop in the remainder of the book.

The deviancy paradigm and pathologisation

The earliest work on stripping developed from a deviancy approach and was resoundingly negative about the activity. Initial accounts focused on women's motivations for working in the industry and pathologised the decision to enter this 'deviant occupation', accounted for by focusing on the 'salient social, psychological and physical characteristics' (Skipper and McCaghy 1970: 391) of the individuals. Whilst the criminological focus on strippers during the 1960s and 1970s did move away from examining stripping as 'crime' to that of 'labour', this is a range of criticisms at the limitations of the earlier works. Bruckert (2002: 14–15) delivers the most succinct criticism, noting three key shortfalls in the deviancy paradigm. Notably, one charge is the obsession with sexuality. This included early sexual activity, the absence of a father figure and a 'tendency towards exhibitionism' (Skipper and McCaghy 1970: 403; see also Carey et al. 1974). Criminologists concerned with deviancy focused on the 'career contingencies', that is, the intersection of particular experiences, moments and opportunities that led to dancers' 'eventual emergence as full-blown systematic deviants' (Skipper and McCaghy 1970: 391). This attempted to understand the 'deviant behaviour' of stripping by contextualising it in time and space and found that characteristics that were evident amongst dancers included 'first ordinal position in the family; early physical maturation; early coital experience; absence of the father from the home by adolescence; and early independence and departure from home' (Skipper and McCaghy 1970: 395). In particular, the criminologists emphasised the location of almost 90 per cent of dancers as the first born in their family, although they offer no indication of why this might be the case.

It is indicative that many of the now significant number of articles published on the stripping industry have been (and continue to be) published in the journal *Deviant Behavior* (cf Thompson and Harred 1992; Rambo Ronai and Cross 1998; Erickson and Tewkesbury 2000; Brewster 2003; Morrow 2012). Those writing from within the 'deviancy' paradigm systematically emphasise proclivities to exhibitionism (Forsyth 1998) and a desire for attention amongst strippers, seeking explanations for engagement in erotic dance primarily in the identities and personalities of the women (albeit with a nod to financial motivations). Moving beyond the limitations of psychologising individuals and the narrowness of unidimensional understandings of motivations, the early work on stripping and strippers ignored the social and cultural impetus and context for the activity. One major criticism of the earlier works from Bruckert (2002: 15) is the ways in which 'capitalist and patriarchal social structures were inadequately theorized', leaving the symbolic interactionist's guilty of 'astructural bias'.

What was absent in much of the writing on stripping was the subjectivities of the workers and the cultural context in which this work was performed. The introduction of radical feminist writings on erotic dance did little to address this absence. Although taking into consideration wider structural factors such as gender norms and – to some degree – economic compulsion, many radical feminist perspectives on stripping continue to pathologise women working as strippers, albeit differently from the classic deviancy literature. Much of the radical feminist argument that 'lap dancing' is part of the sex industry falls on the basic ideas that prostitution and pornography are the archetypal patriarchal institution which objectifies, subjugates and is harmful to all women in society (Barry 1995; Jeffreys 2009).

impressions of women who strip. Grandy (2008) refers to 'exotic workers' as 'dirty' workers and whilst this is taking from sociological understandings of types of work (Hughes 1958), it ultimately has the effect of re-iterating negative judgements about women who strip for a living. Whilst Grandy illuminates the 'messy' nature of identity construction in her analysis, the prerogative term 'dirty workers' jars with any feminist methodology that place participants at the centre of the research and knowledge production process. Nevertheless, Grandy offers a framework for understanding the occupational micro-analysis of identity formation concluding that 'the process of securing a positive identity [is] complex to manage' (2008: 179). Group interviews with small groups of dancers (twenty-one in total) uncover what Grandy terms the 'psychological barriers' employed by dancers on the job: strategies such as projecting disgust onto others (such as other dancers who partake in rule breaking around contact) in order to minimise the stigma directed at themselves. These strategies are notable because they help to explain in a UK context how dancers manage their 'spoiled identities' through alternative narratives and identity construction.

Yet again the Goffmanesque application of the 'spoiled identity' that labels strippers perpetuates an understanding of their identity through one dimension. Examining erotic dance and dancers only through Goffman's concept of stigma yet again focuses on individuals and dancers as strippers (not necessarily multi-dimensional females) rather than as workers in a specific workplace. As Bell (1994) notes in relation to the 'prostitute body' that is turned into a 'deviant body', so too is the stigmatised stripper turned into only one who strips for men: a deviant body that is psychologically damaged by the constant 'male gaze'. Highlighting isolating experiences of estrangement and stigmatisation, a number of authors only highlight the 'costs' of stripping (Pasko 2002; Philaretou 2006). These usually focus on the psychological consequences of self-esteem and identity for the women and men working in this industry (Reid et al. 1994; Ronai and Ellis 1989; Dressel and Peterson 1982).

In contrast, Price (2008) argues that workers themselves tend to emphasise entertainment and the potential to make significant amounts of money. The variation of experience between dancers is explained in part through the life circumstances they experience before their entry into stripping. Sloan and Wahab (2004) argue this can make the consequences of stripping empowering or disempowering, depending on dancers' social location and life experiences. While this attention to previous or exogenous context is useful in differentiating between dancers and challenging universalistic claims about the meanings and experiences of dancing, conditions inside the club in terms of co-relations, management, discipline and surveillance in shaping power and experiences are not considered. While sociologists have been preoccupied with writing about stigma management, how social identity is negotiated, and the consequences of stigma, Bruckert (2002) has instead understood stigma as a stratifying force on which the labour process is built, resisted, inverted and utilised by dancers.

The continued 'gaze' that falls on dancers has tended to zoom in on dancers' relationships with each other (Skipper and McCaghy 1970; Carey et al. 1974; Reid et al. 1995) and their relationships 'outside' the boundary of the club. Such stigmatisation of stripping work, does not, they show, end at the club door and even those involved in stripping in various ways tend to reproduce stereotypes. Within the club, Price (2008: 382) argues that both strippers and co-workers alike tend to construct dancers in negative terms as heavy drinkers, spendthrifts, whiners, slobs and unreliable: 'The contradiction of greater earnings combined with less prestige is part of a larger paradox of gender … compensation for stigmatised work.' Price claims that this devaluation of stripping work by male co-workers enables the other members of staff to save face and restore a gender hierarchy that works in their interests.

Ethnicity

Whilst this is not an exhaustive account of the expansive literature on stigma, identity and exotic dance, one area that is worthy of commentary is the dynamics of ethnicity and racism in the strip club. It is minority women's experiences of the strip industry which are least heard, with a few texts from sociologists such as Brooks (2010) and Bradley (2008) who have examined the stratification around ethnicity in the strip business. Importantly, particularly in the USA where the strip industry is demarcated specifically along the lines of ethnicity, Bradley (2008) notes that one of the more contemporary trends in the strip club scene is further demarcation of the hierarchy of clubs in relation to race and class. What Bradley calls the 'promotion of the hyper-sexualised ideal', which is based on an American white stereotype of beauty, immediately puts non white women at a disadvantage both in gaining access to clubs and in 'winning' customers. The standardised white image of what a dancer 'should' look like has a negative impact on poor and minority women, which in turn creates exclusionary practices by management (Bradley 2007). Brooks (2010), in sharing her own experiences as a black American dancer who worked at the Lusty Lady in San Francisco during the 1970s when collegial action organised the first union, expands on the ways in which strip clubs in the United States are stratified by racial hypersexualisation. Such stratification on the lines of colour led to what Brooks terms 'racialized erotic capital' as ethnicity becomes a currency traded between managers and dancers and dancers and customers.

In understanding the relationships formed within a strip club, the centrality of ethnicity as an organising principle has recently received further attention from those interested in migrant women (often from the Baltic and Eastern European regions) moving to Western capitals in search of strip work (see Penttinen 2010). The dynamics in the strip club is complex: 'racism, classism, ethnocentricism, and the way in which they intersect with gender and stigma, form the hierarchy of desire at strip clubs' (Law 2012: 142). Discussing stigma and ethnicity in the strip club in a Canadian context, Law (2012) highlights how there is an 'acceptable otherness' of the Romanian female stripper: she offers foreign exoticness yet is white, so therefore is more acceptable to customers and management. Indeed, Law demonstrates how dancers 'cash-in' on this exotic otherness through their relationships with customers and gaining favour with management. This is more akin with the UK demographics of strippers (see Chapter 5), as apart from central documents how tax forms and payments are rarely recorded and that workers are generally unaware of their rights as workers. Egan (2004) argues that this makes exotic dance different from other types of gendered labour, as the informality of the strip club produces these distinct labour relations. Instead, Egan parallels exotic dance with domestic labour and brothel sex work, which tends to operate under similarly informal conditions.

Regulation and rules in the strip club workplace

A focus on rules and regulation of dancers is a common discussion throughout the literature (Egan 2004; Price 2000, 2008; Deshotels and Forsyth 2006). Research demonstrates the ways in which the club and the actors within it are managed through both explicit and implicit rules (Colosi 2010). Explicit rules generally include non-touching clauses which may include 'performing fellatio, hand jobs, or allowing customers to touch their breasts and/or vaginas' (Egan 2004: 306). Other rules revolve around proportions of commission and profits, including providing the club a percentage per service, or agreeing not to sit with a non-paying customer (Egan 2004). Breaking these rules results in consequences such as fines or dismissal, something we discuss in detail in Chapter 4. Other more implicit rules may never be expressed by the club, but instead are communicated and passed between dancers and other workers. Colosi (2010) notes that tacit rules which novice dancers learn are passed on through rituals and routines that dancers copy from each other, particularly in the backstages of the dressing room during preparation time. Such rules can include not meeting customers outside the club, continuously 'working the room', and particular systems of tipping (Egan 2004). Tacit rules tend to focus on the degrees of power that are enabled and limited through the organisational rules that govern the strip club as a workplace. These rules are shown to be extremely changeable and designed, like most systems of regulation within the workplace, to elicit both productivity and docility (Egan 2004).

Some accounts demonstrate the ways in which the rules and regulations limit the autonomy of the dancers as workers. Attention has been paid to the use of surveillance, including both technological and human methods of surveillance (Egan 2004). Price (2008: 367) draws attention to the 'larger cast of club characters who own, manage and work'. In doing so, she identifies the gendered stratifications of labour roles within the club, demonstrating that men tend to own, boss and patronise, while women work and perform. Importantly, she demonstrates the ways in which the other roles in the clubs – bartenders, DJs, bouncers – are designed in order to enable surveillance and discipline of dancers (see also DeMichele and Tewksbury 2004 on 'bouncers'). Their success in their jobs is shown to depend on their ability to monitor and discipline dancers. Interestingly, dancers also tended to discipline and regulate each other's behaviour, due to competition over wages. Although this was not a formal or official part of their work, their personal income depended on it.

Egan (2004) argues that such surveillance produces far more anxiety in the workers than the presence or behaviour of the customer, as it is the opinions and actions of management that can have much further reaching consequences. She argues that three forms of regulating gaze operate within the club: surveillance, self-surveillance and peer surveillance. Working simultaneously, these 'reinforce managerial authority, which becomes saturated throughout the club' (p. 306). Through the use of these multiple sources of surveillance, control can be exercised over dancers without the need for management presence. Sporadic punishments of dancers materialise the surveillance and demonstrate its ubiquity to all dancers and employees in the club. Importantly, Egan demonstrates the ways in which these forms of control, combined with the independent contractor status of the women, result in an extremely unequitable relationship between dancers and management and leave dancers vulnerable.

Price (2008) uses a gendered organisational analysis to examine the functioning of the strip club more holistically. This offers an important contribution by moving beyond interactional analyses of workers–customers to examine the roles of other members of staff in producing conditions and experiences inside the club. She identifies the biggest fault line through the occupations performed in the club not as existing between genders, but between dancers and other workers. This reflected the valuation or devaluation of the other labour processes inside the strip club, as well as gender ideologies which divided women along the good girl/bad girl dichotomy. Understanding the relationships between these roles is important for understanding the larger workplace dynamics, beyond dancers and clients. The role of other workers in disciplining dancers as the key generator of value is important for demonstrating the ways in which 'the rules of engagement are firmly set to women's individual and collective disadvantage' (Price 2008: 380). In contrast, Deshotels and Forsyth (2008) and others (Egan 2004; Colosi, 2010) argue that such organisational structures not only controls and disciplines dancers, but can, at times, also be enabling for women. Other workers can be complicit with dancers, by helping them both to manipulate and control customers and to raise the income of all workers in the club. For example, door staff and security may work with dancers – often in exchange for a tip – by turning a blind eye to forbidden behavior such as prohibited forms of touching or exchanging phone numbers (Egan 2004).

These depictions of the power relations within the clubs demonstrate the ways in which the venues, as products of culture, reproduce the very structures of power and relations from which they emerge (Price 2008). This is useful in placing the strip club in broader, macro-social inequalities of gender, race, sexuality and class. Where the strip club is considered in these terms, weight has tended to fall on macro-structures of gender, to the detriment of race (as noted above), sexuality and class. Finally, an important turn in the literature is towards the analysis of regulation at a broader level, noting how moral regulation and the regulation of bodies determine strip club regulation (Bruckert 2002). Jackson's (2011: 355) analysis of the strip club laws in Las Vegas, Nevada, notes how the erotic dance legislation works to counter strip club culture by 'restrict[ing] sexual expression in the marketplace'. Frank (2002) and Liepe-Levinson (2002) have previously described how

Questions of power are the common thread that emerges throughout this literature, mainly focusing on the negotiation of power between dancers and their customers, or sometimes between dancers, management and regulation. Few of these studies have looked at how the degree of power experienced by dancers is produced over multiple scales, such as management behaviour, organisational rules, local and national regulation, and wider socio-economic factors. Most research has focused on one element of these, tending to revert to exploring how gender norms and sexual inequality are affected at a micro-level.

Although there is a growing body of work analysing the location and role of strip clubs and strip work in macro-economic, cultural and gender processes, these three scales and structures have rarely been considered together. More specifically these have not engaged with questions of the terms and conditions of dancers' labour relations and experiences of work, particularly within specific regulatory frameworks and how these sit in wider shifting political economies of gendered, classed and raced power.

While questions of agency, resistance and power are threaded throughout the literature, this is rarely, if ever seen through a robust labour perspective. There has been a tendency to focus on power and negotiations in the labour *process*, exploring what is being sold and to whom, on what terms. The labour *relations* through which this labour is performed, however, receive somewhat shorter shrift.

We contribute to the literature by specifically examining the UK strip club from a labour/employment perspective, and whilst we incorporate different theoretical frameworks and build on the micro-sociologies that have gone before, our main substantive interests are specifically the working conditions and employment of stripping work. We argue that the literature on dancing still lacks a multi-scalar, holistic approach to understanding the labour performed in strip clubs and that incorporating such understandings of labour process and the labour market are productive for moving beyond relative micro-sociologies of stripping. As such we argue for the development of a framework that can account for internal organisational structures and disciplines, as well as statutory regulation and wider cultural, social and gender norms, which we develop in the remainder of the book.

References

Barry, K. (1995) *Prostitution and Sexuality*, New York: New York University Press.
Barton, B. (2002) Dancing on the Mobius strip: challenging the sex war paradigm, *Gender and Society* 16 (5): 585–602.
Barton, B. (2006) *Stripped: Inside the Lives of Exotic Dancers*, London: New York University Press.
Bell, S. (1994) *Reading, Writing and Rewriting the Prostitute Body*, Bloomington: Indiana University Press.
Bernard, C., DeGabrielle, C., Cartier, L., Monk-Turner, E., Phill, C., Sherwood, J. and Tyree, T. (2003) Exotic dancers: gender differences in societal reaction, subcultural ties and conventional support, *Journal of Criminal Justice and Popular Culture* 10 (1): 1–11.

Bindel, J. (2004) *Possible Exploits: Lap Dancing in the UK*, Glasgow: Glasgow City Council.

Bott, E. (2006) Pole position: migrant British women producing 'selves' through lap-dancing work, *Feminist Review* 83 (1): 23–41.

Bradley, M. (2007) Girlfriends, wives and strippers: managing stigma in exotic dancer romantic relationships, *Deviant Behavior* 28 (4): 399–406.

Bradley, M. (2008) Selling sex in the new millennium: thinking about changes in adult entertainment and dancers' lives, *Sociology Compass* 2 (2): 503–18.

Brents, B. and Sanders, T. (2010) The mainstreaming of the sex industry: economic inclusion and social ambivalence, *Journal of Law and Society* 37 (1): 40–60.

Brents, B., Jackson, C. and Haubseck, K. (2010) *The State of Sex: Tourism, Sex and Sin in the New American Heartlands*, New York: Routledge.

Brewster, Z.W. (2003) Behavioral and interactional patterns of strip club patrons: tipping techniques and club attendance, *Deviant Behavior* 24 (3): 221–43.

Brooks, S. (2010) *Unequal Desires. Race and Erotic Capital in the Stripping Industry*, New York: State University of New York Press.

Bruckert, C. (2002) *Taking it Off, Putting it On. Women in the Strip Trade*, Toronto: Toronto's Women Press.

Carey, S.H., Peterson, R.A. and Sharpe, L.K. (1974) A study of recruitment and socialization in two deviant female occupations, *Sociological Symposium* 11 (1): 11–24.

Colosi, R. (2010) *Dirty Dancing. An Ethnography of Lap-Dancing*, Cullompton, Devon: Willan.

Coy, M. (2010) A brave new world: the strip club ban in Iceland and meanings for gender equality, *Gender and Development* 18(3): 545–7.

Day, S. (2007) *On the Game. Women and Sex Work*, London: Pluto Press.

DeMichele, M. and Tewksbury, R. (2004) Sociological explorations in site-specific social control: the role of the strip club bouncer, *Deviant Behavior* 25 (6): 537–58.

Deshotels, T. and Forsyth, C. (2006) Strategic flirting and the emotional tab of exotic dancing, *Deviant Behavior* 21 (2): 223–41.

Dressel, P. and Peterson, J. (1982) Becoming a male stripper: recruitment, socialization and ideological development, *Work and Occupations* 9 (4): 387–406.

Egan, D.R. (2004) Eyeing the scene: the uses and (re)uses of surveillance cameras in an exotic dance club, *Critical Sociology* 30 (2): 299–319.

Egan, D.R. (2006) *Dancing for Dollars and Paying for Love: The Relationships Between Exotic Dancers and Their Regular*, Basingstoke: Palgrave Macmillan.

Enck, G.E. and Preston, J.D. (1988) Counterfeit intimacy: a dramaturgical analysis of an erotic performance, *Deviant Behavior* 9 (3): 369–81.

Erickson, D.J. and Tewksbury, R. (2000) The gentlemen in the club: a typology of strip club patrons, *Deviant Behavior* 21 (3): 271–93.

Forsyth, C.J. (1998) A deviant process: the sojourn of the stripper, *Sociological Spectrum* 18 (1): 77–92.

Frank, K. (2002) *G-Strings and Sympathy: Strip Club Regulars and Male Desire*, London: Duke University Press.

Frank, K. (1998) The production of identity and the negotiation of intimacy in a gentleman's club, *Sexualities* 1 (2): 175–201.

Frank, K. and Carnes, M. (2010) Gender and space in strip clubs, in R. Weitzer (ed.) *Sex for Sale. Prostitution, Pornography and the Sex Industry*, New York: Taylor & Francis.

Grandy, G. (2008) Managing spoiled identities: dirty workers' struggles for a favourable

3   Empty shell licensing
Law, reform and Sexual Entertainment Venues

Introduction

In April 2010, the Policing and Crime Act (2009) came into effect, changing key components of the licensing of the striptease industry in the UK. These changes had been encouraged by a number of public discourses made up by a variety of voices concerned about either the impact of stripping on their local community or the wider social impacts of sexualised entertainment. In what follows, we review the change in licensing regulations during 2008 to 2012 that are now set to govern the striptease industry in the UK for the foreseeable future. To make sense of how these changes occurred, we chart the different narratives that have been detectable within public debates. These range from narratives centred on assumptions and concerns about crime and anti-social behaviour to radical feminist discourses which contest the activity on ideological and moral terms, claiming the industry is of a broader detriment to all women. We argue that these narratives were given vastly more credence over voices emanating from the industry itself. However, we also argue that it is owners, rather workers, who have been given the most space to speak on behalf of the 'industry'. This enabled the debate to be framed in terms of concerned female activists, on the one hand, set against exploitative industry bosses, on the other, leaving a vacuum around the people most affected: the dancers, whose voices are sidelined in the debates.

In this chapter we draw on empirical data from interviews with dancers and regulation officials (namely police licensing officers and licensing and enforcement officers) to provide new voices within the debate over licensing reform. We argue that this licensing has been something of an 'empty shell' in terms of the core issue of working conditions, which have not been addressed as a regulatory matter, but instead fall through the net in terms of any official authorities that are responsible or accountable for the strip club as a workplace where labour is performed. This review leads us to argue that the reform has left gaps in which exploitative management and unfair practices are able to prevail, leaving dancers on the peripheries, with little labour protection. We point out that despite dancers' invisibility in this context, there is the potential for local authorities to use new powers positively to make changes to licensing conditions that protect dancers' working conditions and well-being.

Narratives of reform: they who shout the loudest

Since 2007, on the back of much political intervention into the laws on prostitution (see Sanders 2012), there have been several dominant discourses on striptease reform. These dominant discourses are unpicked below including: resident's
power and community safety; crime and anti-social behaviour; radical feminist
voices; industry representation; and workers' silence.

Public narrative: residents' power

Over the past decade, the voices of residents, upset over plans to open strip clubs
in or near their neighbourhoods, have been well documented in the media.[1] Dem-
onstrations, bill board posters and objections submitted to licensing committees
represent expressions of one of the more powerful narratives that called for reform.
The ways in which the identity of the 'resident' or 'community' subject operate to
embody greater cultural capital and claims to space in a particular locality became
important. A specific case of residents' complaints in the city of Durham led to
the debate about the 'place' of lap dancing being taken to parliament. In 2007,
Roberta Blackman-Woods, Labour MP (City of Durham), supported local residents in their campaign to get The Loft table dancing bar closed, due to what they
considered its inappropriate location near to the city cathedral.[2] The city council
had originally given the bar a licence as a premise with alcohol and striptease,
but the residents took their case to the magistrates court, where the decision was
overturned, on all four objections under the 2003 Act, leaving the bar without a
licence. This decision was then upheld in the high court. As a result of this case,
Blackman-Woods raised concerns that local authorities and therefore local people
did not have enough powers to be involved in the decisions about the location and
existence of these bars, and she argued that this was an indictment on the rights of
citizens living in these neighbourhoods.

This specific, locally grounded case was the beginning of a national campaign
supported by Blackman-Woods. Her power and influence was lent to the campaign group Object (see below), who, together, worked on the issue of reclassify-
ing what it called 'lap dancing' bars.[3] The MP introduced a Ten Minute Bill into
the House of Commons on 18 June 2008 to reform the striptease licensing laws.
Blackman-Woods stated:

> This is not about moralising. This Bill does not seek to ban lap dancing
> clubs. It merely seeks to strengthen and add to the criteria that can be taken
> into consideration when deciding whether to license one in a particular
> location ... Most of us agree that there are areas in cities where perhaps
> adult entertainment is suitable, but there are areas where it certainly is not.
> My Bill will give local people and local councils more of a say over which
> area is which.[4]

As Blackman-Woods clearly indicates, this approach was chiefly concerned with
an issue about 'who' should be exposed to adult entertainment, relating to debates

Eden 2007:10; Colosi 2013).[7] Eden's claim, which surmised that rapes in the London borough of Camden increased alongside the opening of a strip club, has been widely debunked for mathematical errors and methodological inaccuracy, such as the use of raw numbers rather than examining the rate of occurrence and the impossibility of proof of causation. Analysis of the statistics in fact show a lower rate of rape in Camden when compared to other boroughs with no strip venues (Maganti 2012: ch. 4) and the rate subsequently falling over time in an analysis of long-term trends. The author of the Lilith Report (Eden 2003) simply claims this is because of the presence of strip venues in the areas: yet there is no causal or relational evidence about this link or discussion as to why this would be the case. In addition, it is well documented that there are significant external factors which must be taken into account in any discussion of rape statistics such as attrition, awareness campaigns to encourage the reporting of violence, police recording methods and victim support services (Kelly 2008). A relationship between strip venues and sexual violence therefore cannot be established on the basis of the Lilith Report data (Eden 2007). These claims, which should be taken seriously, since violence against women is an important policy and justice issue, appear instead to be politicised interventions, designed to fuel anti-stripping sentiment and influence decision makers, rather than make evidence-based claims in the interests of all women's safety.

Cultural assumptions that stripping causes crime and disorder have not been held up in official discourses and documentation in the UK. For instance, in the plethora of reviews, reports, consultations, guidance and legislation that have taken place in relation to prostitution in the UK, strip-based entertainment was never raised as an area of concern (cf. *Paying the Price* (Home Office 2004); *Co-ordinated Prostitution Strategy* (Home Office 2006)). At the time of the licensing reform being discussed at government level, the Department of Culture, Media and Sport (hereafter, DCMS) explicitly stated that there were no concerns about the licensing of strip clubs in relation to crime and disorder. Citing evidence given during the parliamentary discussions, a representative from the DCMS stated that the evidence suggested that 'venues are much less likely to cause crime and disorder problems than other late night venues'.[8] The DCMS reported evidence provided by Chief Inspector Studd of the Association of Chief Police Officers (ACPO) which demonstrated that strip venues were seen as 'low risk' in terms of public order. On the contrary, he stated that clubs

> tend to be fairly well run and they tend to have a fairly high staff ratio to customers. The people who tend to go there tend to be a bit older, so they do not drink so excessively and cause the crime and disorder problems.

There was a consensus around this view amongst licensing officials, the 'street-level bureaucrats' who are primarily responsible for enforcing these policies (Hubbard and Colosi 2013). They themselves disabuse the notion that clubs are linked to disorder, particularly when compared to other night-time economy venues:

they're not high on the list of – whereas some public houses … the police literally, if they're not called there for the 999 calls they are going in every Friday because of the problems there. So they're not – in my view, my personal opinion, and … I suppose my experience as well – … problem premises, they're quite professional, [they] appear to be quite professionally run.

(Lisa, licensing officer, northern city council)

Rather than public disorder, licensing officers cited the main types of complaints that they encountered as revolving around disputes over (often very high) bills that have been charged to customers: 'normally the only reason they [the police] are called is because of disputes over the cost of champagne' (James, senior liaison and enforcement officer, northern city council). Another regulator stated that in a year only two incidents had taken place 'both surrounding the issue of bills being paid and neither resulted in any arrests' (Estelle, police licensing enforcement officer, northern city).

CCTV, door staff security and stringent door policies, all required by both sets of licensing, meant that much of the unwanted activity, when it occurs, is managed in-house. Again, complaints tended to emanate from customers:

Every now and then you'll get the odd assault inside. You'll get allegations possibly that door staff are being heavy-handed in removing people from premises when they've had too much to drink or they've been too friendly with the girls.

(Estelle, police licensing enforcement officer, northern city)

Licensing officers referred to a small number of instances of women working without the correct visas in strip clubs. However, immigration officials visit a few times each year as the industry was not judged as a high priority. We attempted to interview a representative from the UK Border Agency but after a year of trying, we were told that there had not been any contact from the agency with the strip industry. We further sought to understand possible links with fraud and financial crimes. Conversations with police officials working in the 'proceeds of crime' team suggested the mundane reality that connections between strip clubs and money laundering were largely the domain of *The Sopranos* drama series. Applicants applying to be the licence holder are individually scrutinised in relation to criminal and civil offences, providing a safety net to weed out any convicted criminals from holding a licence (of any kind). In one large city in the north of England, fraud police officers reported they had found no instances of money laundering that could be proven, despite undercover operations on a few club owners. According to police and licensing officials, then, the suggestion was that, in general, the large sums of cash circulated within strip clubs meant that the strip industry was an all too obvious candidate for criminal activity, and therefore tended to be avoided by organised criminal networks.

Licensing officers and the police thus associated low levels of reported crimes with these venues. These assertions are statistically supported by a Freedom of Information (FOI) request made in 2006 regarding police visits to strip venues (see Table 3.1).

The official demand from Object was not to ban 'lap dancing', but rather to reclassify the activity as part of the sex industry (something the majority of dancers we spoke to in our study vehemently opposed).

Second, intertwining their objections with residents' demands for more control, Object campaigned for tighter regulation which would license strip clubs as distinct from other leisure venues. Object combined forces with disgruntled residents – running action days and gathering support from campaign groups across the country – who had tried to prevent clubs opening up in their neighbourhood. They lobbied for the re-introduction of the 1982 Local Government Act, claiming it would 'give local authorities the power to license lap dancing clubs as Sex Encounter Establishments thereby enabling a much greater degree of control over the rapid expansion of lap dancing clubs occurring countrywide' (Object 2008: 4).

The idea of 'rapid expansion' (or 'growing tide') – that is, that the industry was growing exponentially and spiralling out of control – was a recurring theme of the campaign. However, these claims tended to use spurious data about the number of clubs that had been licensed during a few months in 2008, without attention to the high level of churn in the industry, including clubs that had closed, not been reissued with a licence or changed into other premises. Object demanded that strip clubs be recognised and licensed as 'Sex Encounter Establishments' (because they assessed erotic dance explicitly as sex) under the 1982 Act. In May 2009, the DCMS supported this call to use the 1982 Act to regulate strip clubs. In part, the DCMS recognised that these venues were both similar to and different from others selling alcohol. Seeing 'lap dancing clubs' as a 'hybrid' of the sex industry and the entertainment industry, they argued that such clubs:

> do not fit neatly into either the sex encounter regime or the licensing regime to which they are currently subject. For this reason we do not believe that it is appropriate to treat lap dancing clubs in exactly the same way as sex encounter venues such as sex shops and sex cinemas ... Nevertheless a lap dancing establishment is not the same as a pub or nightclub, and interested parties with legitimate concerns should be able to make representations to the licensing authorities without having to resort to making spurious objections on grounds such as the location of a club's toilets.[12]

This appears to fit with Hadfield's (2007) assertion about licensing policy development more generally: that the DCMS has attempted to balance the interests of facilitating the leisure industry with those of the police, local government and Home Office.

Voices from the industry

Representation from the industry during many of the pre-legislation debates and also within the local authority consultation processes following the introduction of the law largely comprised the voices of only a few 'big players'. During the Select Committee hearings, two representations were made. The first of these was made by the celebrity club owner Peter Stringfellow, who has been an informal representative of the industry for over four decades, and the second by a more recent group, the 'Lap Dancing Association'. The LDA claims to be a representative trade body aiming to 'promote the highest standards of professionalism and responsibility towards staff, dancers, customers and local communities'.[13] Both of these industry 'representatives' gave evidence to the panel based on lengthy work experience in managing clubs and the complexities of the licensing process from the club owners' perspective. They were keen to oppose what they termed 'myths' presented by Object. To counter the claim that 'lap dancing clubs are licensed in the same way as coffee shops', lengthy detail was presented which demonstrated that their clubs are in fact licensed through highly strict sets of licensing conditions and processes. They emphasised the existing array of tools of control that planning and local authorities already had to restrict the numbers of clubs, revoke licenses and close down premises and argued that, in light of this, no further regulation was necessary.

There were significant weaknesses in the evidence in that owners did not demonstrate the professional and formal nature of their business, particularly, for example, by referring to the Codes of Conduct by which they run their organisations internally, or the impact of the proposed legislation on themselves as small businesses and on dancers as independent contractors. Instead these two industry representatives appeared to simply respond to campaigners' claims, rather than bolstering their evidence with good practice and management.

This narrow representation was weak as only two organisations represented the 'industry', with little evidence from independently owned clubs or those outside London. The most significant weakness in the industry representation, however, was the lack of attention given to dancers' experiences. No working dancer was involved in the Select Committee hearings (Object brought a 'survivor' of the industry but there was no counter story). There was no real-life account of working under the existing legislation and issues that were pertinent to their experience as workers in a sexualised environment. This absence of a key stakeholder in the debate and evidence collection set the tone for the 'reform'. Most notably, the Object group failed to take onboard how their campaign would have detrimental effects on the women who worked in the clubs and the sex industry more generally. For instance, their use of language and insistence that 'sex' encounter was a core element of any re-classification ran counter to the general feeling amongst dancers, who saw the label of 'sex worker' as inappropriate and without relationship to their work. Dancers in our study were very clear about the negative connotations of the new, imposed language and label:

> I think they should say 'adult entertainment' because it is entertainment, that's all that's going on, there's nothing else happening, but councils and any other people who are going to pass legislation need to understand that we do need things to change, there does need to be a big change in the industry, but what they're doing at the minute is changing it for the worse, because it's just going to push it underground, because there are more illegal clubs opening where

would mean that there would be more underground events organised by the girls, which is something that's happening a lot more now anyway because girls are fed-up of the high house fees and … are starting to organise more of their own totally underground events.

(Faith, 34, white British)

There is already a detectable unregulated strip scene occurring in London largely initiated by dancers resisting the levels of exploitation by high street venues, which is likely to be expanded further by the processes set in motion by the new licensing regime. This could lead to the development of a two-tiered system: one which is regulated and the other left to self-regulation, more vulnerable to organised criminal activity and poor conditions. In terms of the safety and well-being of dancers, these prospects are alarming. Stripping in venues where the safety of the dancers has not been taken into consideration heightens the risk of unwanted physical contact from customers, limited facilities for dancers, (i.e. no changing rooms or place designated for performers), no one to control the audience and also no one to enforce the rules of engagement, securing dancers' safety. The likelihood of this increases further with 'nil policies', removing dancers from the eyesight of even the enforcers of the empty shell licensing, which at a minimum seeks to ensure basic safety standards.

Dancers working conditions

The narratives that centred on crime and disorder, anti-social behaviour, the objectification of women and the 'sex object culture' entirely bypassed the realities of thousands of women dancing each night in the UK. Legislators were apparently more concerned with the externalities of the strip clubs than the internal conditions for workers inside the club. Concerns about 'community' were constructed by excluding dancers and those who worked in the clubs as part of this community. Seemingly more concerned with unhappy residents and assumptions about criminality than whether dancers are being treated fairly and within the frameworks of employment law, the debates seemed to miss many of the issues that are voiced by dancers themselves. Many dancers were sceptical about the evidence basis for the new laws, feeling that decision makers had little idea about the reality of the industry:

The people that brought this legislation in, you know that they're probably just boffins sat in an office somewhere, probably going 'oh, it's disgusting, they're all being degraded' and it's not true at all, they've probably never stepped foot in a lap dancing club in their lives and if they have they've gone to the worst one. It's just not like that at all.

(Bella, 26, white British)

Dancers we spoke to during the interviews were very aware that they were scapegoats for much wider issues which drowned out their real concerns as workers with no representation:

The industry is now being scapegoated because the real issues that affect vulnerable women like sex trafficking, arranged marriage and forced prostitution are unpopular politically … There needs to be more regulations within the industry, we as dancers have for too long allowed others to dictate to us how we are to perform and interact. What we do is not illegal yet is still seen as a fringe job lacking in respectability and a gateway to prostitution.

(Poppy, 21, mixed heritage British)

Workplace exploitation and poor conditions are extensive in the industry, characterised by fees and arbitrary and disproportionate fines, favouritism and bullying from management, poor facilities, long hours and issues of safety in the workplace (Chapter 4). Poppy argued that instead of the licensing conditions that had been put in place, it would have been more beneficial to dancers to improve conditions that shape their experiences:

The industry requires regulation in order to prevent unfair and unpredictable rules being aimed at workers. There needs to be some form of uniform guidelines with regards to the way in which these places are run. For example: my club does not have a first aid box. As it currently stands, I feel that management ultimately have complete control over workers, it is this which is actually exploitative, not the actual strip work.

(Poppy, 21, mixed heritage British)

In the next chapter we demonstrate how dancers face serious issues in terms of their vulnerability to financial exploitation from managers and owners. Debate around the gendered, precarious and financially exploitative nature of the work itself has been wholly absent in the narratives which shaped the law change. Female dancers were simply not regarded as significant or a key stakeholder for regulatory bodies. In fact, some dancers argued that these new conditions, in particular the increase in the licence fee, would have a deleterious impact on their situation:

The new licensing laws have done nothing to change the way the dancers are charged fees and fined and treated by the owners, in fact they will now probably have to charge the dancers more to cover the licensing cost.

(Ines, 35, Spanish)

In this regard, strip clubs have been treated in law solely in terms of their land use impact on the community and not as a workplace in which employment relations materialise. Throughout the remainder of the book we argue that everyday experiences of work and exploitation for dancers should be part of the regulatory framework and criteria on which premises are licensed. Informed licensing committees have the potential to use their new powers to assess these issues in the clubs they regulate. Under the 1982 law, the local authority has the permission to impose certain 'terms, conditions and restrictions' on the licence. Currently this is stated as regulating opening hours, displays of advertising and the visibility of

Goodey, J. (2008). Human trafficking: sketchy data and policy responses, *Criminology and Criminal Justice* 8 (4): 421–42.

Hadfield, P. (2007). A hard act to follow: assessing the consequences of licensing reform in England and Wales, *Addiction* 102 (2): 177–80.

Hanna, J.L. (2005). Exotic dance adult entertainment: a guide for planners and policy makers, *Journal of Planning Literature*, 20 (2): 116–34.

Home Office (2004) *Paying the Price: A Consultation on Prostitution*, London: Home Office.

Home Office (2006) *A Coordinated Prostitution Strategy*, London: Home Office.

Hubbard, P. (2002) Maintaining family values? Cleansing the streets of sex advertising, *Area* 34 (4): 353–60.

Hubbard, P. and Colosi, R. (2012) *Initial Findings Sexualisation, Nuisance and Safety*, Canterbury: University of Kent.

Hubbard, P. and Colosi, R. (2013) Sex, crime and the city: municipal law and the regulation of sexual entertainment, *Social and Legal Studies* 22 (1): 67–86.

Jackson, C. (2011) Revealing contemporary constructions of femininity: expression and sexuality of strip club regulation, *Sexualities* 14 (3): 354–69.

Jeffreys, S. (2008) Keeping women down and out: the strip club boom and the reinforcement of male dominance *A Journal of Women in Culture and Society* 34 (1): 151–73.

Kelly, L. (2008) Contradictions and Paradoxes: International patterns of and responses to reported rape cases, in G. Letherby, K. Williams, P. Birch and M.E. Cain (eds) *Sex as Crime*, London: Routledge.

Magnanti, B. (2012) *The Sex Myths: Why Everything We're Told is Wrong*, London: Orion Books.

Mai, N. (2010) *Migrant Workers in the UK Sex Industry: Final Policy Relevant Report*, ISET, London Metropolitan University. Online: www.uknswp.org/resources%5Cpolicy findingsMigrantsinUKSexIndustroct09.pdf.

Object (2008) *The Growing Tide: The Need to Reform Licensing of Lap Dancing Clubs*. Online: www.object.org.

Pantiniotis, J. and Standing, K. (2012) License to cause harm? Sex entertainment venues and women's sense of safety in inner city centres, *Criminal Justice Matters* 88: 10–12.

Sanders, T. (2012) Policing the sex industry in P. Johnson and D. Dalton (eds), *Policing Sex*, London: Routledge.

4 The race to the bottom

Working conditions and value production in the strip club

Introduction

Much of the anti-'lap dancing' campaigning has focused on the facades and signage of clubs, concerned with the effect that the club has on the surrounding area and particularly on women walking past the premises (the resounding image being that of the young mother forced to wheel her pushchair past exotic dance establishments) (Patiniotis and Standing 2012, Hubbard and Colosi 2013; see also Chapter 8). In this classic construction of the 'Madonna' versus 'Whore' dichotomy of womanhood, in which the Mother is constituted as the subject deserving protection, with the right to exist in urban space, what has been missing are the actual material conditions of work for the women working inside the clubs. In this chapter we explain how clubs operate in relation to dancers, beginning with the multiple ways in which value and profit is extracted from them. We first address the dancers' status as self-employed independent contractors and the disciplinary mechanisms which are used to control the dancers such as house fees, commission and fines. Next we highlight the physical conditions of the clubs, which – with notable exceptions – tend to be unsatisfactory (particularly behind the scenes) and, at times, dangerous. We propose the notion of a 'race to the bottom' as defining the current occupational culture of the strip industry, in which competition and financial exploitation incentivises undercutting and supplying 'extras' to customers. We conclude the chapter by arguing that it is these conditions of work which have partially contributed to the expansion of the stripping industry in recent years as clubs are able to make significant profit directly from dancers' fees, while shifting much of the financial risk to the dancers (see also Sanders and Hardy 2012).

Profit is generated within the club from several sources. Clubs receive income through door fees for customers (usually between £5 and £20) and drink purchases (largely by customers, but also by dancers) from the bar. Conspicuous consumption of overpriced drinks is an important cultural element of practices within strip clubs, particularly in high-end clubs in the capital and major metropolitan centres. Bottles of beer and champagne can cost up to twice their normal cost than in a standard bar, club or restaurant. As Jackie, the dancer manager of a chain of 'gentlemen's clubs' stated, 'we don't really sell pints of beer and all that sort of

A dissection of the technicalities of this case in terms of establishing if the dancer had a contract as defined in law has been explored in detail elsewhere (Cruz 2013). Legal experts have not agreed on whether or not the obligation in clubs amount to a contract of employment and legal scholars argue that the legal status of 'worker' may be more appropriate for dancers (p. 11), while the broader issue of the mechanisms of control clubs/managers have over dancers still remains. Yet, as Cruz notes, had Quashie been deemed an employee, the effect may have been to force clubs to employ dancers with contracts; this may not, as she points out, be welcomed by the dancer community. As our own study found, dancers opt for working in the industry primarily to be free from 'normal' contracts of employment obligation and instead to enjoy the flexibility of the work and relationship. Cruz (p. 14) reminds us that 'sex workers have vigorously campaigned for the right not to be told how to do their work, whom to do it for and under what conditions; sex workers want to remain "unmanaged"'.

Despite the complex legal arguments over determining employment status in strip clubs, due to the level of control clubs have over dancers we argue their work is structured by a 'myth of self-employment', in which dancers adopt the financial risk of paying to work in a venue, regardless of the level of custom, but have numerous elements of their work controlled by management. We have described elsewhere how these rules can be categorised by four different types: procedural, behavioural, interactive and financial (Cruz et al. forthcoming). Taken together, these rules signify extensive control over dancers' labour and behaviour inside the clubs. Below we outline the main mechanisms of control and methods of extraction of value that make up the 'myth of self-employment' in the form of working hours, house fees and fines.

Working hours and control over shifts

Key to definitions of self-employment is individuals' control over their time. Club managers frequently highlighted the flexibility of stripping work as a key advantage for dancers (as did dancers themselves – see Chapter 5). Dancers could generally pick the shifts they wished to work, although in some of the larger clubs, women were required to work a Monday or Tuesday night in order to secure more lucrative shifts at the end of the week or weekend. Although days could generally be selected, dancers had less control over the hours worked. This meant that they had to arrive for work at a specified time and were usually unable to leave before the end of the shift, even when there were few customers in the club:

> You had to work from 8 o'clock 'til 6 o'clock in the morning. Sometimes you could go in at 10 o'clock, but then you had to stay all the time. So I was going in in the dark and then coming out at sunrise and then having to sleep all day and missing my entire day and I really lost track of my make-up career when I was there, because I was so tired and you had to do a certain number of days and they didn't give a shit what you were doing outside of work. They try and

make out it's alright, but when you ring up and say 'I've got a photoshoot, I can't come in tonight' they just give you a mouthful and I couldn't be bothered with it.

(Bella, 26, white British)

On quiet nights, when few customers had come into the club, dancers often asked to leave early. However, management would frequently force them to stay until the end of the shift (usually until the early hours of the morning). This was at no extra cost to the club, and consistently providing a variety of dancers worked in the club's favour. Some dancers were also charged a 'fine' if they insisted on leaving earlier than closing hours. This lack of prerogative over working hours is suggestive of the fact that management had considerably more control over their labour than may be expected of someone in conditions of self-employment.

Dancers were also required to request holiday time and book time off. In some cases, dancers reported paying a retention fee for their slot within the club, if they wanted to take longer than two weeks' holiday. Pubs, rather than clubs, in particular appeared to be guilty of this practice. One interviewee described how some clubs and pubs had introduced new, more stringent rules around holiday, amongst other issues, over the last few years:

When I started … we could go on holiday whenever we wanted. It was really nice, it was really easy. And then suddenly she started to have these rules, like if you want to go on holiday in August, January, New Years' Eve or something, or no, before Christmas, you have to pay £50. If you go on holiday for more than three weeks, you have to pay £50 and it's like, I'm not an employee. I don't have national insurance. I don't have any security. It's not like in the future I can prove that I worked for this amount of time for this company, so my only advantage is that I can go on holiday whenever I want.

(Gabriela, 32, Spanish/Venezuelan)

Gabriela highlights the contradiction here in which dancers are considered not to be employees for the purposes of tax and insurance, while managers exercise significant control over the temporalities of their work.

House fees, tips and commission

Key to the operation of the clubs was the payment of house fees from dancers to the club. It is these, we argue, that have led to the quantitative growth of clubs and also produced the 'race to the bottom' by encouraging clubs to rota as many women as possible, increasing competition between dancers. Colosi (2010: 31) reveals in her auto-ethnography of Starlets that dancers experienced 'fluctuating and unreasonable house fees, fines and contractual agreements', with very little recourse. It was dancers' status as independent contractors which meant that clubs were able to extract a fee from them, as dancers were paying to rent space in which to work in a similar way to hairdressers (Sanders et al. 2012), personal trainers and taxi drivers.

We have argued elsewhere that one way in which standards have changed is in terms of 'deskilling', in which women are not expected to have dancing, pole or gymnastic skills but are hired for their aesthetic (Sanders and Hardy 2012). Nina and others felt that even these aesthetic 'standards' had been loosened in order to open up the industry to a greater number of women. In doing so, dancing, which previously had been the reserve of models and professional dancers, had become a realistic possibility for many more women, further increasing the labour supply (Chapter 5).

In addition to guaranteed revenue from house fees, clubs also charged commission on private dances and VIP time. These two revenue streams guaranteed the clubs an income, while also extracting value from dancers. Technologies and people nominally designated for security, such as CCTV and doormen, were used to enumerate the number of private dances or VIP time that dancers' sold in order to ensure that the correct amount of commission was paid. Commission was usually set at around 30 per cent, although managers would occasionally raise the percentage if dancers had made a lot of money on one particular night. Dalia reported one incident on the Friday before Christmas – the busiest night of the year, when:

> This girl did 160 dances and they let her dance all night and didn't say a word to her. At the end of the night they said to her, 'you've been dancing dirty, you're not getting a penny of it'.
>
> (Dalia, 20, white British)

In this case, they used the rules and regulations apparently designed to protect dancers and also remain legal to refuse to pay dancers and withhold all the income she had generated.

In addition to these two formalised flows of money from dancers to clubs, dancers offered a further subsidy to the club in the form of formal and informal payment towards other members of staff in the club. It was not unusual for dancers to pay £10 to the 'housemum', thereby paying the wages of one of the management team or to each contribute £1 towards the DJ fee, lowering overheads for the club itself. In addition to this, unofficial systems of tipping were often generated, in which dancers tipped doormen and waiting staff in order to win favour, such as having high-paying customers directed towards them. While some reported tipping managers and others because they'd 'had a good night' (i.e. made a lot of money), it frequently operated as a key part of systems of power and favouritism within the club.

Fines

Fines were used against women apparently to control women's behaviour, although in some places explicitly to extract money from women. Sixty-one per cent (n = 88) of women had been fined at some point during their employment in dancing. Common offences included: being as little as five minutes late (£10–£20); leaving early; not turning up to shifts (£15–£100); not going on stage or not going on in time (£20); chewing gum or in possession of gum (£10); being drunk; using or even having their mobile phone on the 'floor' (£5–£40). In terms of appearance, respondents in the survey reported they were fined for a 'dress being too short' or 'spent too much time doing my hair'. Not paying the house fee immediately could also result in a fine. One dancer reported being fined for 'touching the floor', this rule was enacted in order to stop dancers bending over while naked, which was deemed to be against the licensing rules and many reported being fined for being too close to customers. Others reported non-financial penalties, such as being denied work for seven days after missing a shift or removal from the more lucrative weekend rota.

The use of fines varied between clubs, and some of the larger chains did not fine dancers, as the high level of labour supply meant they simply did not allow dancers to work again if they were considered to have broken rules. Fines and their enforcement were dependent on individual management styles:

> It's just like certain clubs, if you do anything, it's a fine. The club I'm at now, they're like really slack, it's really good. We can sit on the floor with our phones. At [previous club] you get fined for that.
>
> (Poppy, 21, mixed heritage British)

Some dancers experienced a correlation between the size of the club and the degree to which fining rules were enacted. Heidi (26, white British) said that, '[bigger] places ... kind of had these rules and they stuck to them, but in the smaller places if you were a few minutes late they'd be like "don't do it again"'. Some managers appeared to use fines arbitrarily to punish dancers they did not like and show favour to others. One survey respondent said she had been fined 'for missing my slot on the pole, but really it was playing chess with the manager, who was the housemum's husband'. Another reported that one manager who was challenged on heavily fining dancers responded that he was doing it because he 'wanted to buy a Ferrari'. In a time of recession, fines were also increasing. Matilda reported that new fines were being introduced that had not previously been in place. For example, whereas dancers had previously been able to leave the club whenever they wanted to, they were now fined if they wanted to leave before club closing at 4 a.m.

In addition to direct financial contributions to the club's profit, dancers were often expected to provide free labour by engaging with promotional offers such as 'Two for the Price of One' dances, providing free stage shows, promoting the club outside, travelling around in club cars (usually limousines or stretch 'hummers') or even 'flyering' around the vicinity to attract custom. Such activities often also brought them into conflict with the public, other business owners and councils, and under the new licensing rules, some councils (such as Leeds) have banned direct promotion. This is, however, more directly related to the desire to reduce the visibility of clubs in the city centre than a disposition against the provision of dancers' free labour.

Figure 4.2 Board displaying rota of dancers in a strip pub. Photograph by Liz Lock

There's a lot of competition in the club, but because it's so fierce, you don't always make any money. But now I'd almost prefer to go home without any money or a little bit down but where you know you're not compromising yourself or putting yourself in a dangerous position.

(Dalia, 20, white British)

The 'race to the bottom' was largely denoted by work intensification in the form of breaking rules that were in place relating to touch and the degree of sexual contact that dancers could have with clients. This was generally referred to as 'extras' or 'dirty dancing':

There's three times, four times, as many girls working on a night which makes it mega competitive and I suppose they just think I've got to get like an edge up on everyone else. I need to do a little bit more to make a bit more money.

(Matilda, 24, white British)

Well, you can't make money. If the girls in there give someone a blow job for forty quid and you're saying look, I'll get naked for you and you can't touch me for twenty quid – who they gonna choose?

(Poppy, 21, mixed heritage British)

Katy (25, white British) reported dancers being asked to leave due to breaking the rules and subsequently being allowed to return, as they made significant amounts of money for the clubs. As Matilda described, where customers knew or saw that other dancers would offer more for the same money, pressure was put on other dancers to offer similar services:

> I've walked past booths where girls are literally snogging guys and you're looking in and the guy who's walking with you is seeing that. And then I panic that they're going to try and do that to me because they've just seen that with someone else.
>
> (Matilda, 24, white British)

Matilda said that she thought this was having a circular and cumulative effect:

> I've seen more and more girls that weren't doing extras before, doing it because they see all the other girls doing it and they fear that if they don't do it, they're not going to earn money anymore.

Other dancers claimed that it was competition between clubs, as well as within them, that led to this intensification. Sex, they said, was available in 'other' clubs (not in the ones in which they work), which made it harder to attract custom to their club and earn money through non-contact striptease:

> In [another club in the city] there are so many girls doing extras that nobody wants just a normal dance. In there it is like £160 for a shag. It used to be £260, but because of the credit crunch, it has gone down. Here, we charge £260 an hour for nothing!
>
> (Una, 29, Estonian)

Frequently, migrants were singled out as being responsible for providing 'extras':

> There's lot more Eastern Europeans. Some of the other girls don't like it, the rumour is that they do more, but I don't know if that's true or it's just something to do with being against someone who's from another place.
>
> (Nina, 26, white British)

> Some of them don't speak any English. Those that have been around longer speak good English, others are fresh off the boat. It's the same with the Brazilian girls. I think the hustle works better for them, less talking. They just go and put their boobs in their face, or their leg between their legs. The more contact you give in asking for the dance, the more likely you are to get the dance.
>
> (Ines, 35, Spanish)

Indeed, there was a very uneven geography of rules, which was influenced both by the geography of different local authority licensing conditions (this was particularly problematic in London where rules changed by borough and therefore one street could have different rules to another) and by differing levels of enforcement by the club management themselves. This had a symbiotic relationship with the level of enforcement from regulators. As Matilda reported about a club in the Midlands:

> I think because the council is quite strict, they have to be quite careful so if – if they ever thought that a guy was touching you or you letting them touch, they'd be down on you straight away.
>
> (Matilda, 24, white British)

She thought this was positive, as it meant that none of the dancers could get away with providing extras and initiating a downward spiral. Such enforcement was important for precluding the conditions necessary for developing a race to the bottom. Poppy emphasised the importance of club security in enforcing rules, as they tended to have more authority, as this conversation between Poppy (21, mixed heritage British) and Olive (21, white British), two dancers in a large Northern town suggest:

> *Poppy:*   What I like in [northern town], [is that bouncers] go around and they say 'don't touch the girls' and the guys know, because if you say it they're like 'oooh whatever'.
> *Olive:*   They think you're like, teasing them, or whatever.
> *Poppy:*   They see it as a challenge.
> *Olive:*   'She says no, but she means yes'.

Importantly, many dancers felt that the downward spiral of conditions also led to a poorer quality of 'product' or 'experience' within the clubs, both for dancers and for their customers. This was particularly the case for 'professional' dancers who felt invested in the occupation, particularly those who worked in strip pubs in London's East End:

> Managers, but girls as well, I think people should have a broader idea about what performance and entertainment is. It's not just picking an R and B song and taking your bra off. It's not about, I'm going to make £20 out of you now. It's got to be how can I make my place look better? How can I make my dance better? Should I have a performance night with maybe a choreographer, so maybe have some sex shows. Lighting. Sound system. Treating people with respect and if you make a good show people will come back. It doesn't have to be expensive … I see more and more girls who are interested in dancing or stripping, but they have nowhere to go, because it feels a bit dodgy or a bit sleazy.
>
> (Gabriela, 32, Spanish/Venezuelan)

Dancers such as Gabriela who were more career-minded in relation to stripping had concerns that many dancers and managers thought only in the short term about making instant profit. The intensity of focus on the temporary production of profit, they said, either from dancers or customers, left little 'entertainment' value in the industry.

In the face of declining standards and possibilities for income, increasing competition within and between the clubs, dancers had little recourse to insist on changing the conditions. The situation in the wider economy, characterised by a lack of good part-time work, falling real wages and the rising cost of marketised education, in contrast to the relative high wages, or the idea of relatively high wages in the stripping industry, meant that there was a seemingly inexhaustible supply of dancers into the industry. This led to clubs frequently treating dancers as disposable labour:

> They don't care how many get – like how much the girls are going to earn and how many girls are going to get pissed off. Because they know there's always another girl that's going to come in and replace them.
>
> (Matilda, 24, white British)

> We are sadly, very much two a penny. There's no room to do what we do anymore. There's more and more girls looking to do it.
>
> (Julia, 25, white British)

The notion of disposability is important in this context as women had very little power to challenge decisions since managers would simply retort that there were plenty more women willing to take her place. Colosi (2010: 31) describes how a group of dancers rallied to discuss strike action as they were incensed by the attitude of managers and the inconsistency of enforcing 'dirty dancing' rules. Yet the familiar 'scare tactic' was turned on the dancers in this scenario, as the manager threatened to sack them stating there were plenty more dancers to take their place. Due to the constant supply of labour, few clubs or management displayed loyalty towards individuals, but rather accepted a high turnover of dancers, due to the ease of their replacement.

Conclusion

In this chapter we have outlined the changing conditions of work in relation to the internal operations of the club that can account for the expansion of the industry during the 1990s and 2000s. Due to the financial structures of the industry and dancers being turned into a source of profit in and of themselves, clubs were able to expand irrespective of custom. We note in this chapter a range of ways that value is extracted from dancers, which allows clubs to make significant profit whilst most of the financial risks are shifted to dancers (see also Sanders and Hardy 2012). All dancers were considered self-employed, and this, we argue, is key for the clubs, as it enables them to have minimal financial outgoings, while

5 Professionals, pragmatists and strategists

Understanding labour supply in the
UK strip industry

All the [tabloids] really want to print is poor girl ... you know ... either poor
girl or clever girl. And never, oh unusual girl, human being with ... feelings,
just like everyone else ... They've got like two versions ... Two versions of
the stripper: the victim and the success.

(Vida, 26, white British)

Introduction

Declining earning possibilities, multiply exploitative labour conditions, insecure
income and the stigma associated with the strip-based entertainment sector raises
questions as to why dancers continue to seek work in it. Existing research in the UK
(Colosi 2010a: 65) emphasises high wages as the key attraction for working as a
dancer. Yet this research was undertaken largely before the economic crash of 2008.
Our research took place in the post-crash years of 2010–12. To answer the question
as to why women continue to seek work in such an industry in a period of significant
wage decline, we investigate the labour supply into the industry, examining who
works in it and the reasons they offer for working there. Painting a coherent narrative about dancers is complicated as they are characterised by diversity, not only in
terms of motivation, experiences in the industry and class position, but also multiple
other individual and structural factors which shape their entry routes. Dancers, then,
are marked more by heterogeneity than by sameness. We have attempted to present
a thematic analysis of the variety of people working in the industry and their reasons
for doing so, while remaining cognisant of the differences amongst them.

Polarised debates about whether stripping is a 'career' (Deshotels et al. 2012;
Colosi 2010a) or a 'dead-end job' for dancers (Jeffreys 2008) have tended to colour discussion about women's participation in striptease labour markets. In this
chapter we highlight the divergent (and sometimes overlapping) reasons why
women engage in labour in this sector. In the first part, we examine the demographic make up of women working in the stripping industry. We then present a
typology of dancers, typified by the ideal types of 'professionals', 'pragmatists'
and 'strategists'. In presenting this typology we relate the demographic information to each 'type' demonstrating that the variety of women in strip work reflects
the array of demographics of the dancing community. We suggest that strip work

only represents a 'career' (professionals) or a dead-end job (pragmatists) for a minority of women, whilst for the majority of dancers (strategists), strip work comprised one of many life strategies for future-orientated aspirations and desires. Finally, we examine what scholars have defined as the 'non-economic' drivers for engaging in dancing.

Who are the dancers? Demographics in the UK stripping industry

Stripping is a profoundly female, young and single industry. Although the age range spanned from 19 to 39, the majority of dancers (68.8 per cent) in this study were aged between 22 and 29. Interestingly, despite an emphasis on youth within the industry, only 10 per cent were younger than this and over a fifth (21.3 per cent) were older. The age at which most dancers had started dancing was considerably younger, as a large proportion (68 per cent) started dancing when they were under 25 years old and 92 per cent began when they were under 29.

Half of the dancers were single (50 per cent), while the other half were in some form of relationship – 21.3 per cent with someone they lived with, 21.3 per cent with someone they did not live with and 6.4 per cent married. In most cases where dancers had partners, they were aware of their work. Those dancers who maintained secrecy around their work had to engage in high levels of deceit, such as lying about where they worked and concealing the amount of money they earned, or even hiding the cash (in one case behind the boiler in the bathroom) (see Chapter 2 for discussion on stigma and relationships). For others, although their partners knew, few of their friends or family did and they were wary of telling 'people of a certain age for instance, just because the, you know, the connotations it has' (Eerikka, 36, Finnish).

This deceit was a problem for many of the dancers with them reporting that one of the worst parts of dancing was keeping it a secret and not being able to answer an everyday conversation about what you 'do'. Katy (25, white British) said, 'I'm doing my driving lessons right now and I went in the car, he's like "what do you do?" and I'm like "err, I work in a bar" because I can't be arsed with the questions.' This is a familiar narrative across the sex industries (Sanders 2005), but the fact that dancers often kept their occupation a secret from people in their lives suggests that, contrary to claims that dancing has become 'mainstreamed' and therefore more socially acceptable or even desirable, it remains highly stigmatised, leading dancers to engage in secrecy and subterfuge.

While in other parts of the sex industry, pressure groups and researchers have made the case that high proportions of sex workers are mothers (Day 2007), this was not the case in this sector. Only 16.8 per cent (n = 32) of dancers had children, of these, most had only one child (12.6 per cent, n = 24, the remainder, 4.2 per cent, n = 8, had two children). This may relate to the difficulty of finding childcare to cover night-time work, or, that the onus on youth in the industry means that women with children who may have been older would probably have left the industry by the point at which they had children.

cies (see Chapter 1). No agencies agreed to participate in the research project, but Chiara (22, white British) reported anecdotally that agencies took 25 per cent of dancers' earnings on top of club commission, as well as arranging accommodation for dancers, for which they could charge extortionate prices.

The possible disproportionate number of migrants in strip work, as well as in other parts of the sex industry, has led some to assert that 'trafficking' must therefore be taking place with women coerced to work in the clubs (Jeffreys 2008). However, whilst there have been small numbers of sex workers in other sectors of the UK sex industry, such as brothel workers, reporting coerced labour (Mai 2010), without exception dancers in our sample stated that they had never seen or thought that coerced labour was taking place in the clubs. When asked whether they had encountered any examples of forced labour, common responses included:

> No. I think that sort of thing would happen in a brothel maybe but I don't think with dancing that would ever happen. I suppose [I think that] because I've never come across it. I think if they were going to be forced to do anything it would be the full whole works. Dancing is more of a social thing. I've never come across anyone that didn't want to do it.
>
> (Heidi, 26, white British)

Despite anecdotes and rumours of other illegal activities in the clubs, including drug use and 'extras', no rumours of coerced labour were ever reported. Eerikka, a 36-year-old Finnish dancer, even stated that she thought the high intensity of the emotional and attentive labour performed by the dancers made coercion an impossibility, as 'the logic is you can't make any money if you do it against your will'. This view was reflected by a variety of other dancers: 'it'd be pointless forcing someone to go and be a stripper because they wouldn't make any money' (Julia, 25, white British). The general consensus was that dancing and any form of coercion were highly unlikely because of the public nature of the work: 'No, I've never met anyone who I thought was being forced to do it ... sex trafficking and and dancing is so worlds apart' (Anna, 27, white British). As such, aside from the legal and regulated nature of the clubs, frequently dancers referred to the labour process itself as precluding coercion. Matilda (24, white British) said that although she'd never 'got the impression that anyone was forced into doing it', she had 'seen girls that ... do all sorts, but I think it's for their own accord'.

There is evidence that the rhetoric associating stripping with trafficking has been translated into policing activities. For example, raids on nine clubs took place in Ireland where 105 dancers were arrested, the majority being from Eastern Europe. However, 'none complained of being forced against their will to either enter the state or to participate in the dancing' (Ward and Wylie 2010: 175). Whilst many informal economies are either criminalised or located on the margins of legal economic activity, our research revealed no evidence, anecdotal or otherwise, that strip clubs are recipients of trafficked women or of coerced labour. Indeed, findings from our project suggest that because of the high levels of regulation and scrutiny under the Licensing Act 2003 and beyond, there was no reported evidence of forced labour or trafficking in the clubs that were included in the research.

Beyond 'money, money, money': trajectories and engagement in stripping work

In her comprehensive monograph on the stripping industry in the United States, Barton (2006) argues that key to understanding dancers' participation in the industry is 'money, money, money'. Indeed, money was cited repeatedly by dancers as their key motivation. Frequently when asked why they worked in dancing, dancers looked askance and simply replied 'money'. In response to an open-ended question about their motivation for starting dancing, 52.1 per cent simply replied 'money'. However, the need to earn money in order to survive in a wage economy underscores all activity in the labour market, and indeed most of our fundamental social relations in capitalism. Since all workers work to earn money, accepting this answer at face value tells us little about the 'social meaning' (Zelizer 1995) or utility of that money. This section therefore explores the differential role that 'money' played for dancers in the study.

Dancers found it difficult to talk about average earnings, due to the inconsistent nature of their income and one dancer, Bella (26, white British), said that money was an intensely private issue amongst dancers. In a highly competitive internal market, dancers – even those who were friends – were in a heightened state of rivalry with each other to secure income (Chapter 4). It was, in general, a zero-sum game. Dancers either gained customers or lost them. Although dancers often had strategies for working together in order to secure income, dancers never shared money or entered into pacts. In addition, money was seasonal. Even in the summer, dancers told us that they were waiting for Christmas, the busiest time of year.

Although dancers considered stripping offered high rates of pay, they were eager to discount the notion that stripping was 'easy work'. Many said that the emotional labour took its toll (see also Barton 2006) and that the intensity and late nights made it difficult, yet the potential for money and the actual money earned tended to override this:

> It's emotionally draining. Because you have to be like 'happy as Larry' the whole time and I don't know, it's demoralising sometimes, coming out with no money. But at the end of the day, you can come out and be like ten times richer than you were the day before.
>
> (Bella, 26, white British)

Leaving clubs without having generated income was demoralising for dancers, because not only is working for pay inherently alienating (Marx and Engels 1844) but also most people depend on a wage for the means to survive and a basic standard of living. Working for no pay (a common experience as 70 per cent of dancers responding to the survey said they had left a shift not earning any money) is an intensification of this alienation. However, despite the idea that money is the most exchangeable, unmarked 'impersonal instrument' (Zelizer 1995), money in fact has multiple meanings. These meanings are contextually and contingently produced, shaped by dancers' class, age, future orientation and aspirations. For many dancers the money earned in dancing had a very specific purpose – paying for education, paying off debt, to send home to their family or alternatively to purchases luxury goods or engage in practices of consumption, either in the night-time economy or of goods outside it.

The social meanings and material uses of the cash-in-hand money of stripping had different resonance with dancers. We discuss these in terms of a seven-point typology. These ideal-types included 'Professionals', 'Pragmatists', 'Avocation-alists', 'Accumulators', 'Students', 'Careerists', and 'Moonlighters'. The first three tended only to work in dancing, though this was for conspicuously different reasons. In contrast, 'Accumulators', 'Students', 'Careerists' and 'Moonlighters' used dancing *strategically*, instrumentalising their work in dancing to meet other aspirations in terms of security and class mobility. They tended to combine danc-ing with other activities including education (15.5 per cent (n = 27), other types of work 26.7 per cent (n = 54) or both other work and education 11.9 per cent (n = 24)). Accumulators also used dancing strategically, but tended to work solely in dancing as a way of generating capital. It should be duly noted these categories represent ideal-types and some women crossed categories and exhibited features of more than one type.

Strategists: students, careerists, moonlighters and accumulators

Common to narratives around women's engagement with dance were the notion of the 'five-year plans'. This was the idea that women would enter dancing, accu-mulate money or other forms of capital for long-term prospects or pay for train-ing and education, which got them onto a career trajectory that they desired. At this point the plan denoted that dancers would leave the industry. Aside from the personal plans to leave the industry there was also 'push' factors which meant that stripping for a living was not a long-term option. Stripping work often has diminishing returns, both economic and personal (Barton 2002, 2006; McCaghy and Skipper 1974; Sweet and Tewksbury 2000) and the importance of youth and body aesthetics automatically curtail the length of time which women can remain in the industry. In this sense, the narratives around many dancers' engagement were generally strategic and time-limited.

The flexibility that dancing offered was widely cited as a key advantage of working in strip clubs. Within the sample, 85 per cent (n = 151) cited the ability to choose their hours as a key advantage or motivation for working in striptease. For these dancers, this flexibility was essential for dancers who were instru-mentalising stripping work to achieve other goals and aspirations. Below we divide the strategists further into four types: students, careerists, moonlighters and accumulators.

Students

Students are increasingly part of the labour supply of strip venues, particularly in cities where there is a large university population. Almost a third (28.7 per cent (n = 50)) of dancers responding to our survey were students engaged in some form of education. Rather than selecting dancing as a career post-education, many women were in fact using it as a strategy to support themselves through further and higher education.

> I first started dancing when I was 22 and that was to fund my degree from university, which was make-up artistry. Which was expensive to do and I didn't know how to fund it and a couple of my friends were dancing and I started.
>
> (Bella, 26 white British)

A key reason cited for involvement in stripping work amongst students was the flexibility it offered in enabling women to fulfil the requirements of their course and earn sufficient income. A Finnish dancer, studying for a Masters, had started dancing when the company she worked for went bankrupt. She said she liked dancing because:

> it gives you flexibility mostly; it can give you the money so you actually have more time. I can't think of any other job that I could do that would allow me to study or yeah – it's – because there is none, because you can't live. There's nothing – you can't get no money from anywhere to survive.
>
> (Eerikka, 36, Finnish)

Similar to other research that asserts the short-term nature of sex industry involvement (see Lantz 2005), many students said that they would stop dancing once they got a 'real' job – defined as a full-time job in their chosen career. However, many student dancers also continued dancing once a week in order to boost their income, which they often found to be insufficient due to the growing mis-match between graduate status and employability.

As Standing (2011) argues, people are being 'sold' more and more credentials (degrees, diplomas and so on) in order to succeed in the labour market. One option is to 'get further into debt to buy the next round, which might just be enough to make the total investment worthwhile' (p. 70). Indeed, the Confederation of British Industry (CBI) (2011) estimates that by 2017, 56 per cent more jobs will require graduate-level training, increasing the need to gain ever more (expensive) qualifications in order to access the mainstream labour market. Although undergraduate students made up the largest proportion of dancers in education, a significant number were taking private courses. Qualifications necessary for moving into professions such as beauty, fashion and make-up artistry were common amongst this group who were paying for non-traditional education. Unlike university education, dancers taking these courses were not eligible for educational loans.

The links between sex work and higher education identified in the study reflect similar findings in Australia (Lantz 2005), France (Duvall Smith 2006) and the

UK (Roberts et al. 2007, 2013; Sanders and Hardy 2014). Roberts et al. (2010) has referred to the 'sexual economy of higher education' to signify the intertwining of the sex and educational markets. Calculations by Roberts et al. (2013) suggest that between £103.1 and £355.2 million per year is entering the UK higher education economy via student sex work.

The links between neo-liberalisation, precarious work and the precarity produced by engagement in education in the context of shrinking state support become ever clearer, raising the contradiction between the privatisation of education and the concurrent vilification of sex work in the UK. Roberts et al. (2010) have referred to the difficulty in avoiding a correlation between student sexual commerce and the (re)modelling of students as customers and consumer of educational services. With tuition fees for higher education a permanent feature of many young people's lives, the everyday phenomena of students seeking part-time work whilst studying, and the flexibility that stripping affords, it is possible to predict that this form of cash-in-hand work will become ever popular amongst female students for the future.

The strong cohort of student-dancers in the sample, and as a key feature amongst the dancer community in general, indicates the class dynamics of some dancers. Determining class through educational status (increasingly so as universities in the UK charge up to £9,000 per academic year), we surmise that there is a middle-class female contingency amongst the dancer community, as dancers were both current students and graduates. It was not necessarily poor/working-class migrant women who were working in the UK strip industry either. Able to mobilise resources to travel and live in the UK, migrants told us they had left permanent stable jobs in their country such as librarian, teacher and nanny to seek more financial rewards through dancing in the UK.

Careerists

While students worked in dancing to fund educational opportunities, others wanted to use dancing to support their movement along the particular career paths they had chosen. Thirty per cent of respondents said that they felt that dancing helped their careers. These *careerists* included Anna, who worked in photography and wanted to make that her main source of income but currently supported her career through dancing. There were other dancers who were pursuing careers in art and other types of creative work, acting and performance and life coaching. Stefania said:

> I have a project at home, I can't talk about it in Romania. I have this project as a sexual health advisor, sexual therapist, so I always choose a really faraway place. I come for a short time, so that they can never find me, by the time they find me I am back at home again.
>
> (Stefania, 39, Romanian)

As job security and possibilities for mobility have been eroded in other more 'middle-class' jobs, as they are 'precaritised' (Standing 2011), other areas of precarious work, such as stripping, become spaces of labour outside 'career' spaces of

employment within which to regain upward mobility. This is particularly important in the context of the growing phenomenon of unpaid internships as a basis
for entering labour markets. This is not simply 'portfolio' working; it does not
constitute doing different work for different employers within a selected career
area (Cohen and Mallon 1999). Instead, precarious labour is instrumentalised in
order to enable career development in another area. Indeed, far from the 'bounda-
rylessness' of portfolio working, these practices instrumentalise strict boundaries
between different areas of work.

Stripping work has often been dismissed as 'not a good career' choice for women,
making a misplaced distinction between 'progressive' jobs and 'static' jobs (Standing 2011), in which the former offers the opportunity for progress and upward
mobility and the latter offers no such opportunities and does not develop a workers'
skills or chances. Dancing has been dismissed as 'static' due to the lack of opportunities attached to it and the limited possibility for mobility. Yet these findings
show that a more complex understanding of the relationship between these forms
of work, 'careers', flexibility, precariousness and stability needs to be addressed.

Moonlighters

Other women were dancing to supplement low wages in their chosen careers that
were insufficient in ensuring women's subsistence or ability to live decently.
Wage declines in real terms, such as those currently experienced in the UK (ILO
2011), have the potential to increase the occurrence of moonlighting in informal
jobs, such as those in the sex industries. Women working in other occupations
included careers in beauty (16.7 per cent), performance (11.1 per cent) as well as
teaching, social work and dominatrix work.[1] In reference to a friend who worked
as a nurse, Heidi (26, white British) explained, 'I think nursing is not very good
money. She works really long hours. She can earn what she earns in a week perhaps in one night.' Some dancers also remained in retail (9.7 per cent), hospitality
(9.7 per cent) and administration work (8.3 per cent), but these types of work were
usually discussed as short term, rather than career paths.

Accumulators

Another mode through which dancers engaged strategically was by attempting to
accumulate capital in order to eventually create income security. Buying property
with a view to producing income as a landlord was a key strategy used by dancers to secure more stable finances in the future and to leave dancing permanently.
Many dancers, particularly those who started before the economic crises began,
had a number of houses and were largely able to live from the proceeds. This was
significantly more unusual with newer dancers, who were more focused on the
short-term cost of living. Gabriela (32, Spanish/Venezuelan) was typical of this
attitude towards dancing, as she said that she planned to 'invest half of it. You
know, I'm going to tuck it away. I'm going to buy a house.' Having property
and money saved was also helping some women weather the financial storm, as

to make changes within the industry. Although, as previously outlined, it was rare for dancers – except in strip pubs – to make money from dancing on the pole, pole work was important to many dancers' enjoyment of their work:

> I really enjoy pole dancing. I love it. It's really good fun. It just looks so good and you know, it's a buzz when people are like 'you're a really good dancer' and you're like 'thanks!'
>
> (Anna, 27, white British)

Avocationalists

In contrast, 'avocationalists' (Snyder, 2004) had little attachment to an occupational identity in stripping, or to a workplace identity more generally. They tended to be more invested in their pursuits outside work and dancing acted to enable the lifestyles that they sought. They liked the flexible nature of dancing for the lifestyle it afforded them, often reflecting the – all too often misplaced – romanticisation of the precarious worker as 'a nomadic subject without fixed roots' (Scanvengo et al. 2007: 106):

> I don't want to be tied down. I want to travel the world … I want to be a yoga teacher. I love doing my make up, I still do my photo shoots. I just can't do a job … It's like, whose life is this? Is it mine or is it yours?
>
> (Bella, 26, white British)

This group of avocationalists were young (under 30) and child-free, with limited commitments that defined the contours of their everyday lives, or their future aspirations. Other dancers echoed these narratives, stating that they preferred to live in the present and respond to changing circumstances: 'I don't have fixed ambitions, I never say, this time next year I wanna do this. I prefer to tell myself oh I'm just, I'll just follow my instinct and see what happens' (Stefania, 39, Romanian). One dancer compared dancing to making commission in recruitment jobs and the 'kick' that they got from working in that way: 'it's a buzz. You get a sale, it's like winning, it's like a game' (Gabriela, 32, Spanish/Venezuelan), but added that although it was exciting, it needed to be combined with something more regular and stable. As Gabriela explained, 'in a weird way I kind of like the uncertainty but I … like, you know, that's why it's not my only job'.

Dancing also enabled migrant workers to travel, both to see the world and to earn money in one place, while being able to return home. Stefania had been dancing for five years for six months at a time in different places, returning to Romania each time: 'it's a good way to travel and not on my own money! I am paid to go to these places, so why should I not use this opportunity?' (Stefania, 39, Romanian). The flexibility and high income generated in dancing also enabled migrants to maintain contact with family:

I can go back, see my daughter. If I think about how much tickets were over the last year, I think it would be about £2000. If you worked on a normal basis you just couldn't do it. You couldn't afford it and you couldn't get the time.

(Una, 29, Romanian)

The varied nature of the work and the fact that 'no two days are the same' was part of the appeal – not being condemned to what they saw as the mundane existence of more traditional working patterns. Indeed, the desire for flexibility was partly about resistance to the normative lifestyle of nine-to-five jobs. In this way it reflected some elements of an anti-work culture, as it signified a rejection of the work ethic symbolised in the desire for a clear career path and fixed hours.

Dancing frequently tied in with a desire to travel. As well as migrants, who were able to earn money and return home frequently, other dancers appreciated the mobility that dancing afforded. Sarah (34, white British) had travelled with an agency dancing across the world, including hostessing in Japan, China, the United States, Iceland and Puerto Rico. There was also significant internal mobility, as dancers moved clubs across a town or city or even across regions. As Julia (25, white British) said, 'you can sort of go somewhere for one night and just be like, hmm. Actually I didn't like it there.' This was despite management's resistance to dancers working elsewhere, irrespective of their self-employment status, which meant they were entitled to work in as many places as they wished.

Pragmatists

Some dancers were simply pragmatists in relation to their engagement in the strip industry. For Dalia, a 20-year-old dancer in the north of England, it was a lack of availability of other work that had led her into dancing:

I've been trying to find a steady job for a while now, like a day job and I've given up. I live in a small town, so there's not a lot of jobs going anyway and I know a lot of people who are unemployed and can't find work. So I'm lucky that I can work where I want.

(Dalia, 20, white British)

Using strip work strategically was evident in the narratives of working-class women, where further and higher education was not part of their life story, or within their horizons or aspirations. Faced with low-paid, unskilled work (often feminised), stripping came into play as a viable alternative to service industry work. Equally, the uneven geography of unemployment in the UK, including regional pockets of long-term unemployment mean that for many women stripping work was either better paid or one of few employment options available. For many women, the selection of strip work over other forms of available work was frequently explained as a strategy to escape low paid, routine service work including retail (15.7 per cent), administration or office work (11.3 per cent) and you can be an illegal immigrant, you can, and you can work and you can make money. You can, if you want to take drugs at work if they're not massively affecting your work [although] I haven't taken drugs at work. But I kind of like the fact that you can, you know? I like the fact that you can decide next month I'm not gonna work and you don't have to fill in a time sheet. You know all the freedoms that come with it being in the shadow economy.

(Faith, 34, white British)

For Faith, a highly educated woman in her thirties, who had left a career in journalism to become a professional stripper, far from stigma leading to disassociation, this was part of the attraction. She thought the reason why women were not subject to street robbery or other crimes when they left the clubs with hundreds of pounds worth of cash was 'because the criminal element recognise us as peers, as allies'. Colosi (2010b) describes these attractions to the 'lap dancing' industry as 'anti-work' where the onus is not particularly on making money, but enjoying the offerings of the night-time economy, the transgressive activities that are available and the informalities of working and living at the edge. She argues that the 'fun engaged with in the lap-dancing club often goes beyond the use of humour', which has widely been noted in other workplace ethnographies and instead incorporates elements of 'leisure activities that might be associated with a night out' (Colosi 2010b: 182). Anna (27, white British) reflected these values, saying that: 'It's sociable, I've got lots of friends at work, I go along and I have a chat. Catch up with everyone. And it's easy. It's not hard work.'

Like Anna and Lana, many women discussed working in clubs as being sociable and 'fun' in that they could drink alcohol, as their job mainly consisted of chatting to other women, staff and customers. For some women, however, this was intensified in that although they worked elsewhere in low-paid jobs, this was the only opportunity they had for engaging in this type of night-time consumption. Some said that it was worthwhile dancing even when they did not make any money, if they could get their taxi and house fee paid and have drinks bought for them. This referred in particular to drinking cocktails and champagne and being in an environment that was seen as 'high end'. Since consumption of particular commodities carries cultural and social value, these dancers were enabled to engage in cultural and material consumption from which they would otherwise have been excluded.

Colosi's (2010a: 73) description of this 'anti-work' attraction also includes receiving sexual attention from men. Flattery and flirtation were mentioned by a significant number of respondents who said that they enjoyed receiving compliments about their looks and dancing abilities. As Julia (25, white British) expressed, 'the attention isn't exactly hard to – to take on. The compliments. You know, they're not a heavy burden to carry.' For others, dancing offered a moment of exploration, not only of their own sexualities (see also Wood 2000) but also a form of a social experiment in encounters with others they felt they would not have met. Dancers referred to encounters with customers as being interesting socially and anthropologically:

I thought it was a window to a life and social classes I never would have ever encountered otherwise … You know the whole lot, just the kind of people that kind of live in that on those times because it was a club that opened up, it was open till six o'clock in a morning so it was [a] really late one, so you got a lot of people coming at five o'clock who just wanted to have a drink, all sorts of people that you met that I would've never ever met, from bankers to builders and you know gangsters too, you know, obviously gangsters to doctors or boring people and exciting people and it was just like hilarious.

(Eerikka, 36, Finnish)

In contrast to approaches emphasising the elision of work and leisure, other dancers were keen to press that dancing was purely waged labour and that they kept spaces of work and fun separate:

I don't think all girls take it as serious as other girls. I do take it quite serious, I never go to work and get drunk. I never take drugs or anything. I never socialise with people I meet at work outside work. For me it's very much go there, have an alright time, and come home. I always drive as well, I never drink. But, other girls go pissed out of their heads all the time, whereas I've got no interest in that.

(Heidi, 26, white British)

Associated with the strip club as an ambivalent place, marked by both leisure (the desire and practice of having fun) and work (the desire to earn money and practice of effort), were the relationships dancers forged through sharing experiences and the camaraderie this generated:

It's like any sort of girls though, they're bitchy towards each other, then you crack them, they're generally alright, soft inside. The club that I work at now is predominantly English girls, I actually go to work now and I actually have a laugh at work now. If there's no customers, we sit around, we have a drink, it's like going out on a Friday night.

(Bella, 26, white British)

I've worked offices, I've worked in factories and there's always some sort of problem, but I've always found dancers easy to get on with.

(Katy, 25, white British)

Katy even said that the friends she had made in the club were the best part of the job, since they were 'proper characters, like you wouldn't find anywhere else'. However, in a context of intensifying competition between larger numbers of women for fewer customers and in order to cover their overheads before profit was made, this solidarity and friendship was increasingly difficult (explained more in Chapter 4). Such camaraderie depended on dancers being satisfied with the amount of money they were making.

this job could actually carry a health warning … 'cos it can be awesome, it can be great fun but there's a lot of dark side that you have to keep your head screwed on incredibly tight to miss.

(Julia, 25, white British)

Although most dancers reported receiving compliments from customers the majority of the time, disdainful or critical comments about dancers' bodies were occasionally prevalent: 'one said once "you're too fat to be a stripper" and I just laughed in his face' (Anna, 27, white British). Sexual overtures and aggressive sexual language was also reported, although most dancers said that it was not overly common:

I've had – I remember one guy being so crude, he said something – I can't remember what he said but it was so crude, I went – 'excuse me; I am someone's daughter, I am someone's sister, I'm someone's partner. Don't you dare speak to me like that! That is unnecessary.' And he – he looked really sorry. He said 'I'm really sorry, I don't know what – I forgot – I kind of forgot where I was.' I said 'that's okay. I understand.'

(Gabriela, 32, Spanish/Venezuelan)

Anna compared such treatment of dancers directly to her experience working within the hospitality sector:

[but] waitressing I've had worse experiences with ignorant idiots, just horrible, horrible people who don't even realise that you're there. I hated waitressing … you have to be like you're not there and you're bending over backwards.

(Anna, 27, white British)

This was a repeated theme. Many dancers recounted that while in other parts of the service sector, 'the customer is always right', whereas in clubs dancers had more freedom to respond to hostility. The dancers, in general, were feisty, strong women who tended to rely on being aggressive back to customers and generally holding their own in encounters with aggressive or inappropriate customers. Many responded to aggression with equal aggression: 'It's a really hard job sometimes … When the girls are dancing it's hard to handle the customer, not to just slap him when they treat us badly or try to touch us. We are there to entertain' (Stefania, 39, Romanian). Gabriela said that she had punched a couple of customers who she felt had behaved inappropriately towards her and both Olive and Poppy reported kicking over tables of drinks onto men when they had behaved disrespectfully towards them. In general, there was an understanding that this was as much a feature of the night-time economy (Jayne et al. 2008), as much as strip clubs in particular: 'every so often you get drunk guys, but that happens everywhere' (Gabriela, 33, Spanish/Venezuelan).

These strategies tended to depend on the context and the degree to which the customer has behaved offensively, as Sophie described:

> If someone is rude to me, my strategy is to make as much money out of them as possible. Take them for everything they're worth ... but some people are just idiots and need to be told to fuck off.
>
> (Sophie, 31, American)

Dancers had a series of strategies for handling customers who were not obeying the 'no-touch' rule. The response from security differed in each club: in some, though not all, they could be relied upon to support the dancers. In general, women had their own strategies:

> You generally sort it would yourself. I know my own strength and how to deal with them – I keep myself under control and say, well about 70 per cent of them are really nice respectful blokes but you get the odd one who tries his luck and you still have to be nice and positive but say you can't do that, and that's how I handle it and usually they are fine. I have never had anyone who is forceful as they know they would be chucked out. If I did I would get them to leave or leave myself ... they know it's a decent club and they can't get away with much.
>
> (Rebekah, 25, white British)

Bella said that she had never experienced treatment that was bad enough to report customers to management or security. Unlike other dancers, she considered inappropriate behaviour by customers as an occupational hazard, an outcome of the highly sexualised atmosphere fostered by the club:

> Unless it's really bad, I wouldn't bother saying anything. Because it's just the nature of the job. You are walking around in nothing but your underwear, getting up on stage and taking everything but your knickers off. If you don't expect like things to happen, or, you don't want it to happen, you're in the wrong industry. Girls that work in strip clubs are strong-minded women and so, anything like that, they're always going to handle themselves.
>
> (Bella, 26, white British)

Julia and Faith intimated that there were subtle strategies that could be used to avoid difficult situations with customers. It was important to make decisions about what to pursue with management and what to leave, but most importantly to communicate to customers that it was dancers who made the rules. For more serious incidents or crimes, dancers did not know which authorities to report to and they felt disempowered from doing so, disqualified from the standard rights in law due to their identity as strippers:

> even though people just say 'oh you can go to the police', it's not that easy because [dancers] don't think they're going to get the support, because of what they do and they also have to worry about whether they'll get in trouble for what they're doing.
>
> (Poppy, 21, mixed heritage British)

Hardy, J. (2009) *Poland's New Capitalism*, London: Pluto.

Hardy, J. (forthcoming) Transformation and crisis in Central and Eastern Europe: a combined and uneven development perspective, *Capital and Class*.

Hardy, K. and Sanders, T. (forthcoming) The political economy of 'lap dancing': flexibility, precarity and women's work in the stripping industry, *Work, Employment and Society*.

Hayashi Danns, J. with Leveque, S. (2011) *Stripped: The Bare Reality of Lap Dancing*, East Sussex: Claireview Books.

International Labour Organisation (ILO) (2011) *Global Wage Report 2010/11: Wage Policies in Times of Crisis*. Online: www.ilo.org/global/publications/books/WCMS_145265/lang--en/index.htm.

Jayne, M., Holloway, S. and Valentine, G. (2008) Drunk and disorderly: alcohol, urban life and public space, *Progress Human Geography* 30 (4): 451–68.

Jeffreys, S. (2008) Keeping women down and out: the strip club boom and the reinforcement of male dominance, *A Journal of Women in Culture and Society* 34 (1): 151–73.

Lantz, S. (2005) Students working in the Melbourne sex industry: education, human capital and the changing patterns of the youth labour market, *Journal of Youth Studies* 8 (4): 385–401.

Mai, N. (2010). *Migrant Workers in the UK Sex Industry: Final Policy Relevant Report*, ISET, London Metropolitan University. Online: www.uknswp.org/resources per cent5CpolicyfindingsMigrantsinUKSexIndustroct09.pdf.

Marx, K. and Engels, F. (1844) *Economic and Philosophic Manuscripts of 1844*, Radford: Wilder.

Maticka-Tyndale, E., Lewis, J. and Clark, J. et al. (1999) Social and cultural vulnerability to sexually transmitted infection: the work of exotic dancers, *Canadian Journal of Public Health* 90: 19–22.

McCaghy, C. and Skipper, J. (1974) Lesbian behaviour as an adaptation to the occupation of stripping, in C.D. Bryant (ed.) *Deviant Behaviour: Occupational and Organisational Bases*, Chicago: Rand McNally College Publishing Company.

McIlwaine, C., Cock, C. and Linneker, B. (2011) *No Longer Invisible: The Latin American Community in London*, Queen Mary, University of London. Online: www.geog.qmul.ac.uk/docs/research/latinamerican/48637.pdf.

Palmer, B.D. (2000) *Cultures of Darkness: Night Travels in the Histories of Transgression from Medieval to Modern*, New York: Monthly Review Press.

Roberts, R., Bergstrom, S. and La Rooy, D. (2007) Sex work and students: an exploratory study, *Journal of Further and Higher Education* 31 (4): 323–34.

Roberts, R., Jones, A. and Sanders, T. (2013) The relationship between sex work and students in the UK: providers and purchasers, *Sex Education: Sexuality, Society and Learning* 13 (3): 349–63.

Roberts, R., Sanders, T., Smith, D. and Myers, E. (2010) Participation in sex work: students' views, *Sex Education: Sexuality, Society and Learning* 10 (2): 145–56.

Sanders, T. (2005) *Sex Work. A Risky Business*, Cullompton: Willan.

Sanders, T. (2007). Becoming an ex-sex worker: making transitions out of a deviant career, *Feminist Criminology* 2 (1): 1–22.

Sanders, T. and Hardy, K. (2014) Students selling sex: marketisation, higher education and consumption, *British Journal of Sociology of Education*.

Scanvengo, M., Galetto, M., Lasala, C., Magaraggia, S., Martucci, C., Onori, E. and Pozzi, F. (2007) A snapshot of precariousness: voices, perspectives, dialogues, *Feminist Review* 87 (1): 104–82.

Snyder, K.A. (2004) Routes to the informal economy in New York's East village: crisis, economics and identity, *Sociological Perspectives* 47 (2): 215–40.

Spencer, D. (2008) *The Political Economy of Work*. Abingdon: Routledge.

Standing, G. (2011) *The Precariat: A New and Dangerous Class*. London: Bloomsbury Academic.

Stenning, A. and Hardy, J. (2005) Public sector reform, women and work in Poland: working for juice, coffee and cheap cosmetics, *Gender, Work and Employment* 12 (6): 503–26.

Sweet, N. and Tewksbury, R. (2000) What's a nice girl like you doing in a place like this? Pathways to a career in stripping, *Sociological Spectrum* 20 (3): 325–43.

Vertovec, S. (2007) Superdiversity and its implications, *Ethnic and Racial Studies* 30 (6): 1024–54.

Ward, E. and Wylie, G. (2010) Lap dancing clubs and red light milieu: a context for trafficking of women into Ireland, in G. Wylie and P, MacRedmond (eds) *Human Trafficking in Europe: Characters, Causes and Consequences*, Basingstoke: Palgrave Macmillan.

Wesley, J. (2003) Exotic dancing and the negotiation of identity – the multiple uses of body technologies, *Journal of Contemporary Ethnography* 32 (6): 643–69.

Wood, E.A. (2000) Working in the fantasy factory, *Journal of Contemporary Ethnography* 29 (1): 1–31.

Zelizer, V. (1995) *The Social Meaning of Money*, New York: Basic Books.

Zetter, R., Griffiths, D., Sigona, N. and Hauser, M. (2003) *A Survey of Policy and Practice Related to Refugee Integration in the EU. Final Report to European Refugee Fund Community Actions*, Oxford: Oxford Brookes University. Online: www.brookes.ac.uk/schools/planning/dfm/.

and the production of value within it. Here we elaborate further and argue that not only should this exchange be considered relational in that it is productive of relations, but also that the form the exchange adopts – and the type of attention that is consumed – is produced (and can only be so) relationally. That is, in the dynamic process of inter-subjective engagement between the customer and the dancer.

In interactive service work, the commodity is consumed in the same space and moment in which it is produced (McDowell 2009) and identities (and bodies) are not incidental, but integral to the encounter (Leidner 1991). The interactive nature of stripping work requires the commodity itself to be relationally negotiated in response to the perceived desires of the consumer to create the appropriate form of attention. Importantly, therefore, we argue that the representation of the dancer simply 'objectified' by the customer is inadequate in discussing the nature of production and consumption of erotic dance – and sex work more generally. Such a relational process necessarily depends on *both* objectification and subjectification performed throughout the striptease encounter.

Labour and consumption in stripping work

> I really enjoyed the dancing bit; I'm not really that into like talking bollocks.
> (Eerikka, 36, Finnish)

We analyse the commodified services available to strip club customers in the chronological order by which the dancer performs different types of labour in the course of their interactions: 1) the preparation and maintenance of the body image and the stage show; 2) the 'hustle'; 3) the private dance; and 4) generating repeat custom/gaining regulars. In doing so, we demonstrate the ways in which the services sold in contemporary strip clubs today are increasingly interactive and affective, not just sexually titillating but also generating a normative gendered experience that constantly moves across a 'continuum [of] sex-attention-care', which are the core 'modes of corporeal communication' in the attention economy of the strip club (Precarias a la deriva 2006).

The body image and stage show

The initial interaction between consumer (customer) and producer (dancer) is fundamentally visual, necessitating aesthetic labour from dancers. There is little doubt that a certain type of sexualised female body image dominates striptease, although the particular type of body image is historically and geographically contingent on changing ideals of beauty and attraction (Brooks 2010). Such aesthetic labour is not particular to the sex industry, as the employment of workers in the wider service industries (retail and hospitality predominantly) also depends heavily on actualising 'desired corporeal dispositions' (Warhurst and Nickson 2007: 107).

Much of this labour begins before dancers step onto the floor, or even into the club. Dancing requires significant preparation, including exercise, waxing and dying of body hair, manicures and pedicures and other body maintenance in order to create the 'stripper self' (Fensterstock 2006). This requires not only a considerable amount of time outside the workplace, but also a considerable investment in these beauty regimes (Rivers-Moore 2013).

The aesthetic fundamentals of 'the stripper look' in contemporary stripping is – in general – premised on an Americanised popular culture image of a white, long haired, fake tanned, slender, large breasted woman who takes on a 'dancer persona' (Barton 2007: 587). This involves fake tan to achieve a bronzed look, manicured nails, impeccable hair (often wigs or extensions) and make-up (usually including false long eye lashes), no (or very little) pubic hair or body hair, covering up of blemishes, bruises and scars (sometimes even tattoos) and particularly prescribed clothing. Other studies report on the extreme thinness apparent amongst many dancers, practising obsessive exercise and/or dieting regimes to maintain what is considered the ideal weight (Bradley 2008: 510). Although we found little articulated evidence of this, some managers controlled dancers' body size by asking them to lose weight and constant surveillance and commentary on their bodies. Julia (25, white British) said that because she had 'a bit of a belly' she did not have the 'typical dancer figure' and therefore had been turned down for a job at Spearmint Rhino, although it had never stopped her finding work elsewhere in the five years she had worked in stripping.

Bradley (2008) marks out this 'promotion of the hypersexualised ideal' as one of the key changes to the stripping industry over recent decades. In the United States, she (p. 509) notes how this is visible in the organisation of more professional clubs and the rise of 'the gentleman's club', making the work of a stripper increasingly 'exclusive'. In contrast, in the UK many respondents claimed that the opening up of the industry to greater numbers of women had led to a relaxation of such stringent standards. In fact, in some cases, particularly outside the hyper-corporate large chains, conforming to a stereotype of hegemonic beauty appeared to becoming less essential:

> To be honest, I don't bother with nails, hair, fake tan. I'm not one of them. Quite a lot of the girls spend so much money on nails, pedicures and like spray tans and well maybe not facials, but they definitely get their tans and extensions and all that and, I don't know, I just don't bother.
>
> (Anna, 27, white British)

Although the expansion of different types of strip venues in the UK led to some degree of diversification, aesthetic labour is still a key criteria in both earning a spot in a club and being able to 'work the floor' (see Colosi 2010). One of our interviewees noted the tensions between personal choice regarding appearance and the strategic conformity to an image that was more likely to generate income:

> I don't like the way I look sometimes but I know it earns me money, I don't like being covered in fake tan all the time which is weird and patchy and comes off all the time. I'm not a high maintenance person, but I have to do it. I know a girl who's got her eyebrows tattooed on, her lips tattooed on, botox,

three boob jobs, this that and the other. It's all because of work and she's not happy. She's not done it to make herself feel happy or because that's the body image she wants.

(Bella, 26, white British)

The production of such an image was often alienating from women's own desires for their bodies. Many of the women therefore used 'props' in terms of heavy make-up and hair extensions to produce the 'correct' image within the workplace, one that was often at odds with their everyday image:

To be honest, I'm quite a scrubber outside work. I've got false hair because I tried to make myself look Barbie bimbo like the rest of them. Boob jobs you can claim back on expenses, because they never would have considered them before. I'm even considering getting one and I don't even agree with boob jobs. I'd say 60 per cent of the girls at least have them, you do have to conform to earn the money.

(Dalia, 20, white British)

As Dalia notes, in addition to temporary bodily technologies utilised by dancers for the purposes (mainly) of their work, there were also a number of permanent and intrusive technological modifications which are fairly common amongst dancers and other sex workers (see Fazzino 2013). It has been noted by Barton (2006) in her study of strippers in the United States (and also Wesley 2003), that between 30 and 50 per cent of women she spoke with and observed had undergone breast implants as they were convinced this figure alteration was linked to higher earning potential. Whilst in our study breast augmentation was not necessarily the norm, there were a significant number of women who had undergone this cosmetic surgery, or said they were saving up to buy a 'boob job' (breast augmentation). The bodywork that dancers perform on themselves is intense, continuous and a source of much financial investment, notwithstanding the significant amount of time preparing and adorning the body before each shift in their own unpaid time. This time, as well as economic input, should be taken into account when accounting for the amounts of money earned by dancers.

There were, however, also suggestions that there was the possibility of avoiding this fabricated image and appearing more 'natural' as a means of attracting clients who saw this femininity as 'fake' and were searching for a more 'authentic' body, usually seen as synonymous with a 'real' attentive encounter:

I work with so many girls that are all different shapes and sizes, a lot of them are big, got big bums, some have got saggy boobs. I think girls worry too much about what guys think. All guys really want to see is a girl who's confident and can use their body in a seductive way. They don't have to be a perfect ten and I know that now, so I don't feel a lot of pressure. A lot of girls come back to work after having a baby and they've got stretch marks and they still earn just as good money and I think all guys have their own taste anyway.

I've asked a guy for a dance before and he's said 'oh no, your bum's not big enough' or 'your boobs are too big, I prefer smaller boobs'. I think a lot of the time people think it's just blonde girls with big boobs, fake boobs or whatever … but I normally find that guys go for or prefer girls who are more natural.

(Julia, 25, white British)

Dancers were supposed to represent women who customers did not encounter in day-to-day life: 'it's not about street, it's not about looking like daughters, it's not about looking like mothers, it's about being a fantasy' (Jackie, dance manager, corporate club, southern city). Customers' tastes could therefore transform in the context of the strip club in order to engage with femininities from which they may disassociate in day-to-day life to sustain class respectability, or because those highly feminised, attentive gender relations rarely exist outside the clubs. In this sense, in the strip club, customers could abandon the distinction of taste to which they would conform outside it in selecting a girlfriend or wife (Bourdieu 1984). The identity of the erotic 'other' enacted by, or projected onto, the non-British stripper (Brooks 2010; Law 2012) also attracted customers who desired 'erotic ethnic otherness' (Penttinen 2010). Beauty, whether 'natural' or 'artificial' or 'exoticised', can be understood as value in this context, in that it circulates explicitly in the strip club in exchange for other types of value, namely money capital (Rivers-Moore 2013).

A further technology utilised by dancers is the adoption of a pseudonym. There are multiple purposes for masking one's real name amongst women in the sex industry (Sanders 2005: 127; Selmi 2013). Strippers purposefully adopt another name as part of the performance for the customer and the first step in building the 'stripper self' (Fensterstock 2006: 199). The names are often obviously artificial, such as Emerald, Porsche, Mercedes or Princess. In literal terms these often refer to statuses associated with wealth or expense, or hyper-feminised icons such as Barbie, Angel and Baby. Other categories include animals (Tiger, Kitten, Foxy), or food (Cherry, Candy) – names that are meant to conjure up a certain sexiness, sensuality or indulgence. Names were utilised somewhat ironically, mobilised to emphasise the performativity of the interaction rather than suggest a name with mundane attachments that were more akin to the customers real-life encounters with women. The falsity of the names assists dancers in creating their working persona as well as customers in suspending disbelief (see also Hayashi Danns 2011). For customers searching for more 'authenticity', dancers are then able to reveal their 'real' name (usually another false name but this time 'ordinary' or 'everyday' such as Laura, Emma or Sarah, which appeared to be class, ethnicity and age appropriate) in order to produce a sense of intimacy. Olive explains:

We have stage names, but sometimes we have fake stage names and they think they're dead clever then 'I know their real name' not like their fake stage name. So they're like 'I'm off to see Jessica' and they feel like they're on a different level, like 'I know something that no other customers knows'.

(Olive, 21, white British)

In the everyday high street strip club, the dancers' aesthetic labour is the first form of labour consumed by customers (for free) as dancers circulate around the floor and when dancers perform the stage shows (for free). Dancers are often expected to perform a three- (one song) or six-minute (two songs) stage show in rotation in order to entertain the audience, generate a 'sexy' atmosphere and attract attention from customers, as a means of advertising their labour and availability for dances or VIP services (see also Penttinen 2010). Until recently in some clubs (particularly in Scotland), dancers were paid to perform on the stage (Lister 2012), but these shows are now considered obligatory free labour, with few clubs allowing tipping on the stage. Usually, these stage shows involve some limited form of striptease to partial nudity (topless) as dancers were resistant to perform fully nude. First, because they felt exposed, but mainly because dancers were then 'displaying everything on stage and [customers] are seeing it for free' (Rebekah, 25, white British), providing a disincentive for customers to purchase a private dance. In this sense, this first moment of interaction operates in the more traditionally

Figure 6.1 Physical labour of pole work: only one part of the story. Photograph by Liz Lock

understood flow of attention, in which the producer seeks to attract the attention of a customer in order to make a purchase.

The work performed on stage is a combination of erotic dance, artistic movement and athletic tricks on the pole. While many dancers are highly skilled pole dancers, others simply dance around the pole, using it to spin and lean on during their three-minute dance. Much 'pole work' uses the core strength of one thigh and frequently projects sheer physical strength, rather than a sexualised dance. It is this image, of the objectified, non-distinct body on a pole gazed at by customers, that dominates much of the popular imaginary of 'lap dancing'. In this sense, this process follows the traditional understandings of an attention economy as it is 'only those who succeed in attracting enough attention can participate in subsequent economic interaction which generates earnings' (Falkinger 2007: 268). Yet this is an almost incidental part of their work in high street clubs. Other forms of labour are far more productive of value – for dancers and clubs alike – in the strip club than the sexualised aesthetic labour of the dancer represented in most popular imaginary and in radical feminist renderings of stripping work as simply objectification of women. It is to these other forms of labour, which are intensively and inherently inter-subjective – that we now turn.

Table 6.1 Labour production by dancers during the 'hustle'

Type of labour produced	Dancers skills	Customers' experience
Bodily labour	Pouting lips, flicking hair, fluttering eyes, smiling, gentle touching and caressing and being touched to establish intimacy.	Immediate physical attention which is highly feminised, suggestive of further sexualised interactions if a private dance is purchased.
Aesthetic labour	Presenting the self as a certain body form, type of femininity, adorned in certain cosmetic and apparel. Acting into the role through name, life story or character, verbalised performance of the visual.	Visually pleasing 'beautiful' young women; personal preferences and tastes met in terms of the 'type' of woman they find attractive (blondes, brunettes, older, large/small breasts, non-British women, women of colour).
Emotional labour	Engaging in 'meaningful' conversation, listening to problems, stories, responding with ego massage conversation, feigning desire and attraction. Humour, banter, playfulness, possibly sexualised talk and flirting.	Intense emotional attention, 'care' and engagement from a woman who puts them at the centre of the interaction. Or light-hearted, humorous interactions, possibly sexualised physical contact and communication, which contributes to feelings of being desired and attractive/'special'.
Interactive labour	Dancer engages in reciprocal social conversation, socialising through drinking, humour, possible mutual attractions and sexualised interaction that are part of a dyadic communication.	Experiencing a more 'authentic' experience, something that could be considered 'genuine' interaction, rapport, sexual attraction.

dancer's existence. Others described how customers eroticised the marginalised nature of dancers: 'there is a big stigma around lap dancing and to be honest, that probably helps us a lot of the time. You play the dumb stripper and you make your money off that' (Dalia, 20, white British). Specifically sexualised attention is directed towards the customer, constructing the dancer as desirous of the customer, often facilitated by the 'empty promise' (Colosi 2010) of more intimate encounters or even suggestions of direct sexual contact, perhaps outside the club. Empty promises can also take the form of more emotional intimacy, as dancer's reveal more about the 'real' them or exhibit emotional vulnerability, encouraging customers to do the same.

This 'dramaturgy of stripping' (Pasko 2002) involves a 'cynical performance' (Colosi 2010: 104), the skill of which is developed over time and deployed as sophisticated hustling techniques. Little previous research has focused on the high level of emotional intelligence and psychological labour necessary to determine the desires of the customer in order to orientate and generate the most appropriate mode of attention. Key to 'the hustle' are emotionally and socially intelligent 'readings' of a customer in order to make a judgement about their social status, emotional needs, political outlook and willingness and financial ability to purchase private dances and the type of attention they desire. The 'reading' of the customer is a key skill that dancers must develop to ensure they offer a specifically niche product to each individual customer. Usually, understanding these readings assumed the form of a subtle game, yet some dancers admitted to being more mercenary:

> I remember once sitting there saying to this guy: I'm really sorry, this conversation is not going well at all is it? I have to ask 'cos it's my job. Would you like a dance? And he's like – 'Oh yeah. That'd be great'. Really?! And we'd just had the most awkward conversation ever.
>
> (Julia, 25, white British)

Those novices who do not understand the importance of the 'reading', or fail to hone these skills, would be unable to generate sufficient income to make dancing worthwhile. As Rebekah commented, reading the customer was not just about observing the 'signs' of class (or wealth) status as this did not translate into wanting to spend money in the club and instead it depended on judging a customers' particular affective orientation in that specific moment in time.

Dancers noted that the emotional labour and interactive skills that enabled them to engage with customers and persuade them to buy a private dance were skills that they had transferred from other service sector jobs. Rebekah was trained as a hairdresser and had her own business for a few years before leaving to go travelling, where she took up striptease as a means of making a quick income. She explains how she transferred skills relating to emotional labour from her work in hairdressing:

> Being confident and having good conversation skills, and being nice, even if you are not, you have to come across as quite complimentary ... I don't think

I could have done it without the hairdressing really as you need to hold a conversation. ... Before I was hairdressing, I was pretty under-confident and I had quite bad anxiety and couldn't really speak to many people.

(Rebekah, 25, white British)

The provision of compliments (positive recognition) by dancers to customers represents a mode of interaction common in other forms of service work (which can also be seen to embody elements of an attention economy), but perhaps absent in long-term romantic attachments (e.g. marriage) or everyday, routine life. This was reflected most acutely in the high proportion of married customers visiting the clubs. As such, customers sought hyperbolic gendered attentive encounters which they felt were largely unavailable within quotidian gender relations.

The success (or otherwise) of the hustle is reliant on interactive engagement and communication, that is, the relationality between the customer and dancers. Frequently, this was not only performed by a performative dancer and a passive, 'authentic' customer but customers also performed roles within the context of the strip club environment, often enacting behaviour and identities that they associated with 'the strip club patron':

To be honest, what I found really frustrating was most ... it almost seemed like they were doing a theatre game, so they weren't talking about real things or what they're really interested in or but they were like putting on a role ... and I think most of it was bullshit. There was no – anything real in the talk, so they're just talking air, they're talking nothing.

(Eerikka, 36, Finnish)

Emma similarly highlighted the performances enacted by customers, seeking attention beyond the authentic encounter as she referred to the

hilarious shit they come out with, because they want to be able to pretend. They go in there, they leave their real lives at the door and they have an escapism. It's brilliant, you have great lines. They're a spy, but they're also an investment banker and then they'll end the night by saying 'I've got to go and DJ now' and it's kind of cute, in a way, you just think 'ha, you poor loser'.

(Emma, 31, Belgian)

The 'hustle' is a key moment in discerning and deploying the particular type of attention required in order to convert a potential customer into a sale of a dance or a 'sit down'. This may take the form of desirous attention for those seeking a sexualised encounter, a performance of mutuality and understanding for those seeking emotional engagement or admiration and unblinking deference for those seeking recognition, in particular of social status as a charming, intelligent or entertaining (i.e. valued) subject.

VIP – it's quite a lot of money in one go. You couldn't have earned that doing the dances. But you sell it on the fact that, you lie, basically, you say 'it's a lot nicer up there and you can have your drinks up there' and you know. It's like 'it's nice and private' and 'the dance'll be intimate', but it's not, it just lasts longer.

(Vida, 26, white British)

As Vernon (2011) notes, such a strategy of feigning desire can be dangerous as it can lead to unwanted attention, men who are not clear about the boundaries, and behaviour that is difficult to manage. Julia recognised that suggesting or actually arranging to meet men outside the club should be avoided:

People [customers] will say 'oh, you know, well, how about … we meet afterwards?' And I won't lead people on because I think you know what, you would stand to get hurt if then they see you outside, they might try and grab you or whatever. So again, it's a case of not putting yourself in dangerous situations.

(Julia, 25, white British)

A key aim of some dancers was not only to generate repeat custom from particular customers on one specific night but also to create regulars who would return and become a base source of income for them. In stripping, much like other areas of the sex industry, workers rely heavily on establishing a regular clientele with whom them can solidify an ongoing relationship and therefore a regular income (see Egan 2005 for an astute and thorough explanation of this). Dancers employ a range of labour forms to try to court a customer so they become a 'regular', not least a mobilisation of the 'girlfriend experience' (GFE) similar to that identified in other sex work encounters (Sanders 2005; Bernstein 2007; Lever and Dolnick 2010; Huff 2011; Milrod and Weitzer 2012; Rivers-Moore 2012). This GFE provides attention rarely found in everyday romantic partnerships, as it delivers an 'authentic' performance of mutuality and desire, without the mundane elements of everyday life (domestic labour, disagreements or irritation, for example) (see Egan 2006). Although difficult in an industry in which dancers move around to different clubs and locations fairly frequently, establishing even a few regular clientele is both a guaranteed form of income and easier work: 'the main way we make our money, the main way I've always made my money is from regulars. That one guy a night who you can have wrapped around your little finger' (Dalia, 20, white British). Dalia explains that the ability to gain regulars is not so much based on aesthetic labour or object–subject relations as a performance of mutuality:

and a lot of that isn't looks based … Most of the time you can just sit and talk to them for a bit. I mean some people just want you to dance the whole time and you just do, but especially a lot of regular customers. I mean, I've got a regular customer, who, he feels weird having dances with me now because he's sort of got to know me. So he'll pay for the VIP, he'll pay for the dance, but he won't necessarily have one. I think in a way they almost see us like being a girlfriend. Well not quite a girlfriend, but it becomes about being a different type of relationship, rather than just customer–dancer, it's, it's weird.

(Dalia, 20, white British)

Dalia's description of dancers' performance of 'the girlfriend experience' reflects the ways in which regulars 'consume exotic dance in a vastly different manner than their cursory or non-regular counterparts' (Egan 2006: 13) and require different modes of attention. This is namely because they are invested in an emotional relationship with the dancer. Indeed, as Dalia suggests above, the establishment of a regular relationship may even lead to a de-sexualisation of the exchange. Egan (2006) convincingly suggests that this is dependent on a suspension of disbelief and the framing of these relationships as 'authentic' and meaningful, often resulting in painful experiences for regulars when this fantasy is unveiled as exactly that. The GFE experience performed in such regular encounters take on the same sexual and romantic scripts that are familiar in non-commercial relationships such as gifts and statements of 'fidelity', commitment and trust from customers (see Sanders 2008a; Egan 2006).

In this context, however, the desire for immaterial commoditised forms of attention and recognition clashes with dancers' material motivations:

Most of these guys are quite lonely. They don't have social skills. So for them, we are their friends, I don't think they have much going on, so they're like 'go to a stripclub to see my friends' and we're like 'oh, nice one, £10!'

(Gabriela, 32, Spanish/Venezuelan)

The disjuncture between Gabriela's understanding of the encounter and that of her customer is neatly summarised in the title of Egan's (2006) intricately constructed book *Dancing for Dollars, Paying for Love*. As she describes, these tensions underpin the delicate balance created by the dancers and it is these, when they surface, that can create hostility and even violence (see also Chapter 5).

In order to create and maintain 'regulars', dancers reflected the practices of other sex workers. Once relationships with regulars have been established, dancers encouraged their custom by exchanging phone numbers with them and inviting them to join them (usually when there was little other custom). Poppy had two phones, one of which she used purely for work purposes:

Whenever it's quiet, I'm like … 'do you want to come down?' It just means I have to do no work, I just have to talk to him and to be fair, he can be quite boring. But it's better than 'can I touch you? What are you going to offer me?' Better to have a boring conversation about whatever, than some guy who's trying to feel you up.

(Poppy, 21, mixed heritage British)

In this case, Poppy preferred the 'boring' emotional labour of a regular to the potential sexual harassment and boundary making of a new customer. Yet the continued custom depended on an extended 'empty promise' (Colosi 2010) of deeper and longer-term emotional attachment created through the dancers' per-formance of 'counterfeit intimacy' (Enck and Preston 1988; Egan 2005; Vernon 2011). Frequently, dancers emphasised that although they were comfortable with the most sexualised element of their work – the private dance – the labour required to deliver a sense of mutuality and recognition was the most abrasive:

> If I am honest with you, I am bored of all of it. I'm just bored of the guys. I find them quite needy. Like they want to be your friend and they want you to listen to them. And they want to hold your hand and be like 'how are you doing today?' I find it quite boring … It's bollocks, you know, you just want to be at home watching *Desperate Housewives*.
>
> (Gabriela, 32, Spanish/Venezuelan)

> It's not so much dancing, it's more like sitting with them, drinking with them and that's like a lot more hard work, because just imagine if you got this bor-ing guy and it's like doing an hour VIP with some boring guy.
>
> (Olive, 21, white British)

As reported by Brents and Jackson (2013), emotional responses must be created in the customer and outcomes must be achieved that make the customer feel interesting, sexually, emotionally or intelligently. Goldhaber (1997: no page) argues that day-to-day conversations 'normally must be kept more or less equal if one party or the other isn't likely to lose interest'. Dancers' frequent represen-tation of strip club patrons as 'boring' is suggestive of the sale of commodified attention in order for the dancer (who may have lost interest in the 'boring' con-versation) to continue to feign interest. Ultimately the dancer must 'recognise' the customer in a way that is different to his other daily interactions. Penttinen (2010: 39) notes how strippers who engage in emotion work perform 'listening bodies' simply to earn more money, as one dancer put it during an informal conversation in a club: 'it's like being like a fucking priest'. Penttinen paints a bleak picture of dancers who have no choice but to perform care and attention, trapped listening to the customer in order to make a wage. Yet in our study danc-ers demonstrated their guilt at conning customers by faking the performance of interest and intimacy:

> I'd have a couple of nights in a row where I just didn't do very well and then I'd have a night where I'd deliberately get a bit drunk, 'cos if I was drunk then I could do the bullshit talking and make the money back but then I'd hate myself for, what I felt to be, manipulating the men and leading them on. I'm not interested in that, if I was doing it just for the money, then maybe I'd do that more easily, but remember I had a very good well paid job so I thought if I'm not enjoying my dance work, there's no point in even being there.
>
> (Faith, 34, white British)

For some dancers, therefore, a particular attraction to the work was, specifically, the delivery of such emotional labour.

The attentive economy: relationality, recognition, mutuality

It is worth emphasising that the private dance – the moment most focused upon on theorisations of 'objectification' – constitutes a three-minute spectacle amidst interactions in the strip club which will usually last significantly longer, often up to hours at a time. This may include paid VIP time or unpaid hustling time during which dancers try to elicit dances from customers. Edie (33, white British) a stripper in East London, poses the question: 'If I am viewed solely as an object, then why do the customers want to talk to me?' Intersubjective encounters between dancers and customers in which attention is exchanged are central to the strip club encounter. Hence, for Edie, objectification seems to be a 'one-dimensional way of describing human interaction'. Understandings of stripping simply as men's gaze over women's naked bodies as they perform, impassive, on stage, misrepresents the interactivity of the encounter, as Edie further adds: 'When I'm at work I interact with all kinds of people as a human being.' Such interaction, it should be noted, is characterised, in general, by particular forms of gendered and sexualised attention.

Throughout these different stages of the strip club interaction, dancers perform varying skills, relations and forms of labour. Underlining each of these, however, is relationality and the provision of attention in the form of recognition, mutuality and attention. As Frank (2003: 61) points out, these are sites in which sexual labour is consumed and yet 'contact and sexual release are prohibited and ... voyeurism and conversation are the eroticized practices'. While practices of voyeurism suggest the one-way gaze of 'objectification', a subject–subject relation underscores each moment of this interaction. For this reason, we theorise the strip club as an attentive economy in which all the labour performed is intended to generate recognition of the customer, through the relation (attraction, adoration, acceptance) that is negotiated between customer and dancer.

The gaze and relationality of the strip club is also homo-social, it should be remembered that the relations that are produced within the strip club are not only between customers and dancers but also between customers themselves (see also Rivers-Moore 2012). Unlike other forms of sex work consumption in the UK which tend to be individual, visiting strip clubs is frequently a collective activity (Sanders 2008b). 'Stag dos' and corporate or business entertainment are key sources of custom, particularly for the larger chain clubs. As Sarah describes, visiting strip clubs in groups is a way of socially engaging with each other without direct verbal engagement and generating recognition from their peers, refracted through relations with women:

> if it's not football, or if they don't want to talk about their work, they want to be distracted in some terms. And it's just another form or entertainment, isn't it, for them ... you know ... This way they don't have to talk to each other

Figure 6.2 Physical, emotional and social attention is at the core of the striptease encounter. Photograph by Liz Lock

and also, it helps – helps massage their egos a little bit as well ... There's a lot of one upmanship ... more so in a, like, a jovial way ... they have, like, this thing where they want to see how long they can talk to a dancer without paying anything. They want to, like, show off to their mates as well.

(Sarah, 34, white British)

The relations of homo-sociality that Sarah describes reflect the ways in which the consumption of the attention economy provided by the labour of strippers can act as a conduit for male mutual recognition, or even for mutual recognition between men and women (in the case of the colleagues or partners who attend). As such, recognition and attention are either consumed directly by customers, reflected in the emotional labour and eye contact of the dancer, or indirectly through affirmation of themselves reflected by their colleagues or partners. The ability to attract and to hold the attention of a young (valuable) attractive female body is a key masculinising practice, enabling men to assert their place in masculine hierarchies.

Conclusions: stripping as an economy of attention

Stripping work requires multiple forms of labour, including aesthetic, emotional, physical and sexual labour in order to deliver attention to the customers who desire it. Strip work is intersubjective service work par excellence. Understanding dancers' labour in this way not only identifies the different forms of labour in which dancers' engage but also emphasises its contingency and its inherent relationality. Different type of customers (e.g. regulars in contrast to occasional customers, individual men versus stag parties or corporate groups) demand varying and shifting constellations of labour in order to experience the attention they seek to consume directly or indirectly. This requires high levels of emotional intelligence from dancers in order to 'read' the customer and to establish the commodified attention that is to be negotiated and exchanged. 'What' exactly is sold in the strip club encounter does therefore not just involve multiple forms of labour, but is contingent on the social dynamics of the context, affective desires of the customer and the physical and emotional boundaries of the dancer. It therefore arises from the 'space between' two actors, that is, their relationality, in a particular historical moment and is thus dynamic, changeable and open-ended, subject to constant, shifting negotiation.

Drawing out the multi-dimensional forms of labour that dancers perform in the strip club, we have argued that it is the desire to consume attention and experience social recognition that underscores all these heterogeneous forms of labour. We have demonstrated that the 'hustle' embodies a combination of intense aesthetic, emotional and bodily labour to produce a mixture of 'normal' conversation, flirting, humorous and/or sexualised interaction and that even the private dance itself, through the pivotal role of eye contact, is grounded in the work of recognition. The focus on 'the body' (and therefore objectification) in the politics of stripping have often by-passed the extent of emotional and interactive labour which is at the core of the striptease encounter. Yet it is these inter-subjective relations which represent the core commodity being consumed in these contexts.

Whatever the constellations of labour that is performed, it is *attention* that is the bedrock underlining all these encounters. Not only this, but it is attention from a particularly valued body – young/female/attractive/heterosexual/feminine. Dancers' performance of desire and their role in recognition means that in this context 'it is the desired body of the customers, with the power of money-capital who can convert into the socially recognised subject' (Hardy 2013: 51). The stripping encounter cannot be explained by simplistic renderings of objectification or object (dancer)–subject (customer) encounters, as it is only a subject who can mutually recognise the social subjectivity of another. These desires for recognition, mutuality and desire themselves are constituted by and constitutive of male-gendered subjectivities, which are (re)produced in the encounter through the specific (sexualised/admiring) feminised attention and the recognition that is performed enables the consumption of a commodified experience of social status (Fraser 1995).

References

Abel, G. (2011) Different stage, different performance: the protective strategy of role play on emotional health in sex work, *Social Science and Medicine* 72: 1177–84.

Agustin, L.M. (2001) Sex workers and violence against women: utopic visions or battle of the sexes? *Development* 44 (3): 107–10.

Barry, K. (1995) *Prostitution and Sexuality*, New York: New York University Press.

Barton, B. (2006) *Stripped: Inside the Lives of Exotic Dancers*, New York and London: New York University Press.

Barton, B. (2007) Managing the toll of stripping: boundary setting among exotic dancers, *Journal of Contemporary Ethnography* 36 (5): 571–96.

Bernstein, E. (2001) The meaning of the purchase: desire, demand, and the commerce of sex, *Ethnography* 2 (3): 375–406.

Bernstein, E. (2007) *Temporarily Yours. Intimacy, Authenticity and the Commerce of Sex*, Chicago: University of Chicago Press.

Bourdieu, P. (1984) *Distinction: A Social Critique of the Judgement of Taste*, trans R. Nice, Cambridge, MA: Harvard University Press.

Bradley, M. (2008) Selling sex in the new millenium: thinking about changes in adult entertainment and dancers' lives, *Sociology Compass* 2 (2): 503–18.

Brents, B. and Jackson, C. (2013) Gender, emotional labour and interactive bodywork: negotiating flesh and fantasy in sex workers' labour practices, in C. Wolkowitz, R.L. Cohen, T. Sanders and K. Hardy (eds) *Body/Sex/Work: Intimate, Embodied and Sexualised Labour*, Basingstoke: Palgrave Macmillan.

Brooks, S. (2010) *Unequal Desires. Race and Erotic Capital in the Stripping Industry*, New York: State University of New York Press.

Califia, P. (1995) *Public Sex: The Culture of Radical Sex*, Berkeley: Cleis Press.

Chapkis, W. (1997) *Live Sex Acts: Women Performing Erotic Labour*, New York: Routledge.

Colosi, R. (2010) *Dirty Dancing. An Ethnography of Lap-Dancing*, Cullompton, Devon: Willan.

Doezema, J. (2001). Ouch! Western feminists' wounded attachment to the 'third world. prostitute', *Feminist Review* 6 (1): 16–38.

Egan, D. (2005) Emotional consumption: mapping love and masochism in an exotic dance club, *Body and Society* 11 (4): 87–108.

Egan, D. (2006) *Dancing for Dollars and Paying for Love: The Relationships Between Exotic Dancers and Their Regular*, Basingstoke: Palgrave Macmillan.

Egan, D., Frank, K. and Johnson, M. (eds) (2006) *Flesh for Fantasy. Producing and Consuming Exotic Dance*, New York: Thunder Mouth Press.

Enck, G.E. and Preston, J.D. (1988) Counterfeit intimacy: a dramaturgical analysis of an erotic performance, *Deviant Behavior* 9 (5): 369–81.

Falkinger, J. (2007) Attention economies, *Journal of Economic Theory* 133: 266–94.

Fazzino, L.L. (2013) Altered bodies, engineered careers: a comparison of body technologies in corporate and do-it-yourself pornographic productions, in C. Wolkowitz, R.L. Cohen, T. Sanders and K. Hardy (eds) *Body/Sex/Work: Intimate, Embodied and Sexualised Labour*, Basingstoke: Palgrave Macmillan.

Fensterstock, A. (2006) Stripper chic: a review essay, in D.R. Egan, K. Frank and M. Johnson (eds) *Flesh for Fantasy. Producing and Consuming Exotic Dance*, New York: Thunder Mouth Press.

Frank, K. (1998) The production of identity and the negotiation of intimacy in a gentleman's club, *Sexualities* 1 (2): 175–201.

Frank, K. (2002) *G-Strings and Sympathy: Strip Club Regulars and Male Desire*, London: Duke University Press.

Frank, K. (2003) 'Just trying to relax': masculinity. Masculinizing practices, and the strip club, *The Journal of Sex Research* 40 (1): 61–75.

Fraser, N. (1995) From redistribution to recognition? Dilemmas of justice in a 'post-socialist' age, *New Left Review* 212 (1), July–August: 68–93.

Garnes, L. (2011) *Can't Knock the Hustle: Hustler Masculinity in African American Literature*, USA, Proquest, Umi Dissertation Publishing.

Goldhaber, M. (1997) The attention economy and the net, *First Monday* 2 (4). Online: www.firstmoday.org/article/view/519/440.

Hardy, K. (2013) Equal to any other, but not the same any other: the politics of sexual labour, the body and intercorporeality, in C. Wolkowitz, R.L. Cohen, T. Sanders and K. Hardy (eds) *Body/Sex/Work: Intimate, Embodied and Sexualised Labour*, Basingstoke: Palgrave Macmillan.

Hardy, K. and Sanders, T. (forthcoming) The political economy of lap dancing: intersectional precarities and women's work in the stripping industry, *Work, Employment and Society*.

Hayashi Danns, J. with Leveque, S. (2011) *Stripped: The Bare Reality of Lap Dancing*, East Sussex: ClaireView Books.

Huff, A.D. (2011) Buying the girlfriend experience: an exploration of the consumption experiences of male customers of escorts, *Research in Consumer Behaviour* 13 (1): 111–26.

Jeffreys, S. (2008) Keeping women down and out: the strip club boom and the reinforcement of male dominance, *A Journal of Women in Culture and Society* 34 (1): 151–73.

Law, T. (2012) Cashing in on Cachet? Ethnicity and gender in the strip club, *Canadian Journal of Women and the Law* 24 (1): 135–53.

Leidner, R. (1991) Serving hamburgers and selling insurance: gender, work, and identity in interactive service jobs, *Gender & Society* 5 (4): 154–77.

Lever, J. and Dolnick, D. (2010) Call girls and street prostitutes: selling sex and intimacy, in R. Weitzer (ed) *Sex for Sale*, Routledge: New York.

Lister, B. (2012) *Precarious Labour and Disposable Bodies: The Effects of Cultural and Economic Change upon Sexualised Labour in Lap Dancing*, PhD thesis, University of Stirling.

McDowell, L. (2009). *Working Bodies: Interactive Service Employment and Workplace Identities*, Chichester: Blackwell.

Milrod, C. and Weitzer, R. (2012) The intimacy prism: emotion management among the clients of escorts, *Men and Masculinities* 15 (5): 447–67.

Pasko, L. (2002) Naked power: the practice of stripping as a confidence game, *Sexualities* 5 (1): 49–66.

Penttinen, E. (2010) Imagined and embodied spaces in the global sex industry, *Gender, Work and Organization* 17 (1): 28–44.

Precarias a la deriva (2006) A very careful strike: four hypotheses, *The Commoner* 11: 33–45.

Rivers-Moore, M. (2012) Almighty gringos: masculinity and value in sex tourism. *Sexualities* 15 (7): 850–70.

Rivers-Moore, M. (2013) Affective sex: beauty, race, and nation in the sex industry, *Feminist Theory* 14 (2): 153–69.

Sanders, T. (2005) *Sex Work. A Risky Business*, Cullompton: Willan.

Sanders, T. (2008a) *Paying for Pleasure: Men who Buy Sex*, Cullompton, Willan.

Sanders, T. (2008b) Male sexual scripts: intimacy, sexuality and pleasure in the purchase of commercial sex *Sociology* 42 (1): 400–17.

Sanders, T. and Campbell, R. (2013) Sexual entertainment venue policies: analysing trends, conditions and improvements in dancer welfare and safety *Journal of Licensing* 2 (3).

Selmi, G. (2013) From erotic capital to erotic knowledge: body, gender and sexuality as symbolic symbols in phone sex work in C. Wolkowitz, R.L. Cohen, T. Sanders and K. Hardy (eds) *Body/Sex/Work: Intimate, Embodied and Sexualised Labour*, Basingstoke: Palgrave Macmillan.

Vernon, S. (2011) *The Private, The Public, The Pubic: Striptease and Naked Power in Scotland*, PhD thesis, University of Glasgow.

Warhusrt, C. and Nickson, D. (2007) Employee experience of aesthetic labour in retail and hospitality. *Work Employment and Society* 21 (1): 103–20.

Wesley, J. (2003) Exotic dancing and the negotiation of identity-the multiple uses of body technologies, *Journal of Contemporary Ethnography* 32 (6): 643–69.

Wolkowitz, C. (2002) The social relations of body work, *Work, Employment and Society* 16 (3): 497–510.

Wolkowitz, C. (2006). *Bodies at Work*, London: Sage.

Zelizer, V. (2005) *The Purchase of Intimacy*, Princeton: Princeton University Press.

7 Falling through the regulatory gap

Managing and licensing stripping

Introduction

In this penultimate chapter we examine the relationship between club management and the regulatory bodies that shape the ways in which clubs operate. It
is within the relationship between regulation and management that the working
conditions that dancers experience can be further interrogated. Bradley (2008: 513
our emphasis) argues for the centrality of the club operations in shaping dancers'
experiences: '*where* women strip may be more influential than the *techniques*
of stripteasing in whether women consider their job exploitative or liberating'.
As Bradley asserts, the particular styles of management and rules of engagement
within a club can either foster problems or alleviate particular difficulties for
dancers. In this chapter, we draw on evidence from managers, owners and regulation officials (mainly licensing officers, health and safety personnel, and police
licensing enforcers) to explore how clubs are regulated. We dissect the ways in
which managers use strategies and discourses of corporatisation, professionalisa-
tion and formalisation to distinguish 'respectable' clubs from others, walking the
(self-defined) tight rope between 'saucy' and 'seedy'. We examine how dancers
are explicitly managed, surveyed and regulated in order to draw conclusions about
how these structuring dynamics affect the experiences of the dancers.

Finally, in this chapter we identify how the sexualisation of the female body
becomes explicit in the structural mechanisms of the law and the 'action' and implementation of the law through its operationalisation. We argue here that it is dancers'
bodies, rendered as sexualised bodies rather than the worker bodies, that become
the subject of regulation through gendered law, policy and the internal organisation
of strip work. In doing so, dancers *qua* workers have fallen through a 'regulatory
gap'. Demonstrating the ways in which the licensing process (up until the design
of some SEV policies) has regulated sexual bodies rather than workers bodies, we
set out examples in which the safety, welfare and well-being of dancers has been
considered and included in licensing criteria as an example of good practice.

Managing risk and avoiding disorder

Responsibility for ensuring that clubs were conforming to their licence conditions fell to a number of agencies: council licensing departments, health and safety

officials, licensing officers within the police force, and police officers responsible for the local area. However, it is the local authority licensing officers who sit at the centre of the regulatory process, as it was these actors who visited clubs to check compliance. Basic conditions of the licence related to whether the licence is displayed publicly, whether door staff are working as per conditions, whether underage alcohol sales is prevented, how the club is being advertised externally, whether the 'signing in' book is being completed, and whether there is CCTV and if someone on the premises can operate it (see Sanders and Campbell 2013). In short, the core licensing conditions are, however, related to the prevention of disorder in and around the club:

> We've got a new system in place, a risk-based system and we're trialling a system out, well it's actually in place now. So we now do a risk assessment. We go on a visit to see how compliant they are. So that's one of the reasons why we go and visit lap dancing. Ordinarily we wouldn't necessarily go unless we had a specific reason to do so.
>
> (Adam, principal licensing officer, northern city council)

This process of checking conditions can be considered extremely 'light touch', in that, if clubs appeared compliant, then no return visits were made. Visits were usually arranged in response to a trigger. Triggers could include intelligence from the police, complaints from the public or accusations from people using or working in the club:

> Lap dancing venues will only come up when possibly there's been a number of incidents and then their status from the police will go up. They [the police] will have their problem premises that they've received quite a lot of calls for, or possibly intelligence, information coming from other areas. Then we initiate a visit.
>
> (Lisa, licensing officer, northern city council)

In terms of concrete complaints, these tended to be initiated from the police, whereas complaints from the public tended to be founded in suppositions about the clubs and their activities:

> The common beliefs that we get reported to us from the public are that there are a number of issues, illegal, unlawful issues, money laundering, well prostitution and illegal workers etc. Clearly I've not come into contact or have no experience of any of those three potential allegations other than that's a perception that people outside of the industry, particularly the public, hold.
>
> (James, senior liaison and enforcement officer, northern city council)

As James and Lisa describe, despite the public nuisance and the crime and disorder narratives that have fuelled the call for strip clubs to be re-classified with greater controls (see Chapter 3), in the broader context of the night-time economy, strip venues were seen to be compliant and not a hothouse of crime and disorder by enforcement officials. In this regard, clubs were given 'green' rather than 'red' light status in the police risk 'traffic light' system. Philip (alcohol and crime community safety manager in a northern city council) and other licensing officials said this was because problems associated with violent crime or alcohol-related crime were rarely associated with strip clubs but other venues in the night-time economy.

'We don't mind saucy, but we don't want seedy'

Significant effort from owners and managers was directed into presenting the club and the daily operational management as in control, compliant with conditions and orderly like any serious business. Formal policies, procedures, processes and structures were seen as an important aspect of good practice to the managers. On several occasions owners and managers, when asked about operations in the club, pushed various policies under our noses or we were taken into offices where shelves brimmed with files on drugs policies, health and safety, risk assessments, incident procedures and financial processes. This approach to formalisation was succinctly characterised by Eddie, who impressed that 'we have written procedures for door staff. We have written procedures for dancers. We have written procedures, yeah. I have written procedures for managers as well' (Eddie, club manager in northern city). This emphasis on formality was an attempt to demarcate the 'professionalism' of the business and the above board, legitimate everyday operations of the management. There was a discourse of respectability that emerged from larger chain clubs who frequently impressed their corporate (read: 'respectable') nature in order to differentiate themselves from independent clubs who were considered to be less 'business-like':

> We're a corporate business, we have a structured staff management, senior managers, you know, it is a proper business, and the business has to be successful to support this structure. It's not like the independents who I've said – it's a lifestyle. If they just go home with five hundred quid at the end of the week, or whatever it might be, I've no idea, that's – they're happy. We got, you know, its big business.
>
> (Scott, owner of chain in the Midlands)

'Big business' and large profits was seen as synonymous with respectability and quality. Variation between the standards in clubs, according to dancers, however, showed no such pattern. For many dancers, small, independent clubs were seen as preferable workplaces. The standardisation, rules and inflexibility of large chains were often not seen as desirable as more traditional strip pubs or small, local, independent clubs, even when there was less opportunity for income generation. Ines (35, Spanish) has worked in the industry for over a decade and moved away from large corporate chains because of the pressure of the rules: 'In some places, they have so many rules, you have to do your nails, your hair, your make

Figure 7.1 Offices of a high street club. Photograph by Liz Lock

up, you have to have a long dress. All these rules and they'll put pressure on you how you look.' Pub strip work was considered much more flexible and relaxed despite a reduced capacity to earn because pubs provided only stage shows rather than private dances.

The use of targets in this sector was a reflection of the corporatisation of this industry, and in a way analogous to most other management styles in contemporary capitalism. One male assistant manager of a northern city centre club described his year-on-year targets which led to a focus on ensuring an average spend of £40 per customer upon each visit. This corporatisation and these mechanisms of management reflects practices of measurement and targets which are now almost ubiquitous in business and management styles, making this sector of the sex industry reflect the management patterns in many other more formally integrated parts of the economy.

The function of the 'corporate' status for economic mainstreaming appears twofold (see also Brents and Sanders 2010). First, a corporate aesthetic offers a brand name and style designed to intentionally appeal to those in the 'corporate' world: enticing corporate capital to be brought in by businessmen who have personal and company finance to spend. Corporate strip clubs courted corporate capital, particularly before the beginning of the recession in 2008, marketing themselves as a source of corporate entertainment and disguising payments on the corporate credit card bill, attributing them instead to the more salubrious venue names such as Riverside Café. Directly appealing to this market, one website from the north of England implored corporate customers to visit the club suggesting 'Want to impress your clients? Show them our latest figures.'

Second, a 'corporate' identity also functions as a means of establishing 'respectability' both in terms of attracting 'the right' customer, but also in establishing a good reputation as a safe and secure entertainment venue. This was important for establishing a reputation with regulatory officials: 'The type of client that these places attract is not the type related to alcohol-related violence. They are "well heeled" rather than young guys out on a boozy night out' (Adam, principal licensing officer, northern city council). This approach draws on and reflects class-based governance of the night-time economy, in which venues associated with working-class leisure are subject to more control and closure, while more middle-class and 'respectable' forms are endorsed and enabled (Chatterton 2002). In so doing, corporate clubs assert themselves as more sophisticated and 'high end' than a smaller independent club that may not have the 'upscaled' modern interior or red carpet exterior to welcome customers. Such discourses of 'respectability' reflect the observations of Bernstein (2007) who writes about the turn in the sex industry which overwhelmingly caters for the middle classes (both purchasers and sellers). Individual (female) workers as well as businesses owners have 'upscaled' their products to attract those with disposable incomes and (supposedly) with behaviour which will not attract disorder, risk or incivility, but will instead attract consumers to engage in 'recreational sexuality' in an orderly and appropriate manner.

Narratives that differentiated corporate adult entertainment venues from other 'seedy' sex businesses have created a club hierarchy. Corporate chain clubs were considered by licensing officers to be more professional than independent venues, which perhaps had a more relaxed and informal management style. A senior liaison and enforcement officer for a southern city council distinguished between different types of clubs, stating that chains were more likely to respond quickly to issues of non-compliance but that:

> the independents you do tend to have a little bit more resistance from [managers] shall we say, but that's probably because of financial issues or other such, they don't have the where with all to be able to address the situation quite as rapidly shall we say as some of the other companies do.
>
> (Emma, senior liaison and enforcement officer, southern city council)

Club management differentiated their venues from others in the night-time economy through discursive strategies, which stressed the club's professional status. For example, a zero tolerance approach to drug use was emphasised by all club managers and owners and most stated that such behaviour was grounds for immediate dismissal:

> We've had one or two drug issues, yeah and they're sacked instantly. Well when I say 'sacked' we can't – we don't sack, but they're no longer able to

work in that venue or any other of our venues. Because we have a zero tolerance completely.

(Scott, owner of chain in the Midlands)

Similarly, all managers denied and condemned the availability of sexual services
in their clubs in order to counteract assumptions that strip clubs are a 'front' for
prostitution. This was usually expressed through differentiation from what they
argued were other less salubrious venues. As one male owner starkly put it: 'We
are not about sex. You know, because we're frankly too expensive' (Scott, owner
of chain in the Midlands). He continued that he knew of strip venues where
'relief' was available to customers for forty or fifty pounds, and he used this
to compare the service that customers received in his club: 'You've got to give
them like the service, you've got to make people feel special, we're quite good at
that, the girls are good at that.' Emphasising the sale of emotional and attentive
labour, rather than sexual labour, was one method of distinguishing their own
clubs as more tasteful and therefore legitimate. Indeed one of the largest corporate club owners in the country preferred the term 'table dancing' rather than
stripping or lap dancing, as he felt it implied entertainment of a more respectable
kind.

Managing dancers' behaviour

In addition to procedural formality in relation to licensing conditions, managers
also emphasised their formal bureaucracy in relation to the management of dancers. Multiple managers emphasised the files that were kept on the dancers, with
their details stored including national insurance numbers, home address, contact
numbers, photographs and copies of evidence of their age (passport or driving
license) and sometimes documents that proved their migration status:

> We've got all of their documents. Every single girl. It doesn't matter where
> – where they come from. We need their national insurance number, their
> address. A bank statement to confirm their address. They have their photos
> taken.
>
> (Jodie, assistant club manager, northern town)

> We are very, very thorough with their passports and their work permits,
> because we have to be. We go through all the rules and regulations with them,
> make sure they sign everything, make sure they're old enough.
>
> (Jackie, dance manager, corporate club, southern city)

'Codes of conduct' were the central mechanism for controlling dancers and disciplining their behaviour and failure to conform to the standards set by the Code
of Conduct document resulted in disciplinary action, similar to that of an ordinary employment contract (Chapter 4). The way in which the Code of Conduct
was generally enacted in practice was through either venue managers, or more

frequently through the actions of a 'housemum'. Below we explore further how dancers were controlled and disciplined, despite their self-employed status.

'Care', control and surveillance

As outlined in Chapter 1, some clubs employ a 'housemum' who is responsible for managing dancers and facilitating their work throughout the evening. Although not explicitly considered management, housemums have an important role in managing and controlling the dancers. They often operate within the changing rooms (spatially, the domain of dancers, rather than management). In addition to collecting house fees, they disciplined dancers for non-adherence of rules relating to appearance or behaviour. Altercations between dancers were also frequently resolved by housemums. Housemums were almost without exception female and were occasionally ex-dancers. The job was highly maternalised, not only in the obvious sense of the name adopted by this role or that they consistently referred to dancers as 'girls' (this was ubiquitous), but also in the sense that housemums were expected to be an 'iron fist in a velvet glove', delivering both care and discipline simultaneously. One housemum, who worked under the more explicit job title of 'Dance Manager' mainly because of the size of the club and number of dancers, explained her role:

> To make sure the girls are dressed properly, that's my main [job]. Then to mark their dances and their money. You might say – well I only say that's my main, the dress business, because that comes first, but the actual – most important is make sure I collect all the house fees and the money that's due because that's the club's money. And obviously, it's the way the girls would act during the evening, that they go on stage and they are nice to the customers, and everything, really, that they don't do dirty dancing and – just you've got to have eyes in the back of your head ... I audition for my own girls from start to finish, I find the girls, audition them, clothe them, help them, train them, given them accountants, give them all sorts of things from start to finish, and that's how we do it.
>
> (Jackie, dance manager, corporate club, southern city)

While some housemums emphasised their caring role, Jackie is more explicit that her key role is in the extraction of house fees, which is considered to be 'the club's money'. Jackie's detailed discussion of her job demonstrates the ambiguous role of housemum. Even the seemingly nurturing element of the role – ensuring dancers are looked after, have the right attire and are 'trained' to the standards of the club – however, is arguably also in the interests of the club. Maintaining quality control and adherence to licensing rules operates as much in the interests of the club as making sure that the women have everything they need for their shift. There is also a more obvious policing role bound up with the role of the housemum because she is the member of staff who checks, enforces, takes money, surveys the dancers and ultimately is in control of whether they can work in that venue again.

Occasionally, they also fulfilled an additional role of negotiating between dancer and customer when transactions did not go smoothly: 'if they don't pay, she [the housemum] tries to go in there and say, "look Sir, come on, the lady danced for you, you should pay her"' (Jackie, dance manager, corporate club, southern city). The feminised nature of this exchange, imploring rather than enforcing payment, although imbued with more authority than dancers, was seen as preferable to the more forceful authority of a male manager or doorman, which could disrupt the affective atmosphere of the club.

In clubs in which housemums were not used, general managers organised dancers alongside their operational duties. This meant that dancers tended to be less 'managed' than where a housemum was present. In these scenarios there was less maternal 'caring' considerations given to dancers – they were expected to turn up with all of their kit and get ready to work a full shift without someone looking after them. In these cases, although the surveillance role carried out by both the manager and the doorstaff was prominent, in reality the dancers had more freedom as there was less of a managerial gaze on their activities.

The corporatisation of the clubs, namely the attempt to produce a luxury or 'high-class' experience, also meant dancers were heavily controlled by the management. For example, dancers' personal hygiene and appearance was closely monitored and managed:

> If they [other managers in the chain] have any issues with a dancer, I go round the clubs and then we confront them and sort it out. It could be just things like saying, could you please get the roots of your hair done, you know, trust me, or could you wear a stronger deodorant, that happens.
>
> (Jackie, dance manager, corporate club, southern city)

In addition to corporeal control, managers were also responsible for directing dancers' labour by occasionally asking them to perform 'line ups' or 'walk rounds' the room to entertain the customers (in the larger establishments), especially if the atmosphere was seen to be waning and not conducive to consumption. Dancers were sometimes pressurised to work outside the club, handing out promotional materials and vouchers, encouraging customers into the venue. Activities of the dancers were monitored (for instance, smoking and rest breaks, who the dancers were speaking to). One club even had the motto 'If you can't make a dance, make a friend' (in reference to the customers), as dancers were encouraged to constantly interact with customers (see Chapter 6 for details on 'the hustle'). While necessarily relationally produced between dancer and customer (Chapter 6), the production of intimacy with the dancers was monitored and managed by managers who would offer advice on interacting with customers and on conversational techniques.

These high levels of control of dancers' labour should be placed in the context of their 'self-employment', offering further evidence of the mechanics of the discipline and control they faced. The social interactions of 'making a friend' involved intense emotional labour which was performed for free for the clubs' benefit, even when dancers would not generate any custom from doing so as danc-ers were not paid for this hustling, nor were they compensated if the time spent with customers did not turn into earnings from a private dance or VIP session. The adage that 'time is money' is of literal truth in the strip club and therefore time spent with customers represented further risk on behalf of dancers, while clubs gained from the free labour provided through the production of an affective environment conducive to the prolonged consumption of drinks, if not dances. Equally, a club full of 'happy' chatting people, as dancers perform their emotional labour with customers, is a more conducive environment to entice other customers in and to stay for longer and spend more on drinks and food.

The relationship between management and dancers

Clubs and managers differed significantly in relation to their attitudes and rela-tionships with dancers. Understandings of power permeated through the man-ager–dancer relationships. Despite the high levels of control outlined above, some managers were suspicious and even fearful of dancers, suggesting that they held all the power in the relationship, as the functioning of the business depended on them. This was in stark contrast to the feelings of disposability experienced by many dancers, a notion which may even be generated by management from the knowledge that clubs depended on dancers for income. Many club owners demanded strong distance between managers and dancers:

> You can't mix with the girls. I've had to get rid of two managers from this place because once you mix with the girls, no matter how good you are, this place goes down and there's got to be a kind of a line between you and the girls … I treat it a bit like an army camp because you have to, because females can dominate men, yeah.
>
> (Eddie, club manager in northern city)

The notion of powerful women, that 'females dominate men', meant that there were segregation policies in many clubs, not only with dancers and managers but also with DJs and doormen. Women's sexual appeal, the very basis of accumula-tion within the club, represented a serious threat to order and the accumulative strategies of the business by its potential to co-opt male staff to dancers' own interests. Other staff's role in surveillance of dancers (such as door staff 'marking' dances so the club can keep tabs on the amount of commission to charge), made this particularly dangerous. For this reason, 'flirting' within the club was forbid-den. While 'flirting' may be a subjective judgement, relationships between the dancers and staff were strictly forbidden:

> I have this policy here, and I've had it in all the clubs, yeah, any member of male staff gets involved with a dancer is a dismissible offence instantly, without a warning – go instantly. And basically on a Saturday night I've taken a doorman off the door and I've sent him home because I've found out he's

been sleeping with one of the girls. No questions asked, and that's it. He's gone.

(Eddie, club manager, northern city)

As in all management relationships, a hierarchy of control existed between dancers and managers (Price 2008) and dancers frequently reported being 'talked down to' by the managers. For some managers, this was a specific tactic of control:

It's difficult when you've got 35, 40 girls a year on a night time, trying to control them all … The girls will only do the job properly if they're scared of you, they like you or they respect you. So in that occasion, yeah. So a certain few of them, they like the management, a certain few respect the management, and a certain few of them are, like, scared. And what I mean by scared is like I've got a female manager and all she does is, yeah, she walks round and fines the girls.

(George, club manager, northern city)

Fining then, as George describes, was not simply used as a punitive tactic for rule contravention but also for establishing relations of control. Such authoritarian styles were on occasion even considered necessary by some dancers: 'I do feel sorry for managers a lot of the time too, having to look after however many girls and they're not all angels, some are a nightmare and some do get hammered and cause a bit of a scene' (Heidi, 26, white British). For Heidi, the need to ensure control over the dancers and accumulation of profit for the club in a context of alcohol consumption and an atmosphere grounded in hedonism and excess justified authoritarian management strategies.

Turn-over of dancers was highest in clubs with strict and authoritarian managers, as dancers had little emotional loyalty to the club. High turnover could also create hostile working conditions and since dancers valued freedom and flexibility (Chapter 5), they would take their labour elsewhere. High turn-over of dancers was not considered an issue by managers due to the abundance of supply – particularly in areas where there was a large student population (see Roberts et al. 2013; Sanders and Hardy 2014). This made management unwilling to listening to any concerns or desires to improve working conditions. In fact, high turnover could be seen as beneficial, as it meant a wider pool of dancers for customers to choose from (also see Colosi 2010).

Dismissal was not always the first resort of managers and a dance manager from a corporate city chain explained that they would find alternative arrangements: 'Some girls aren't allowed at certain clubs because they've fallen out with other girls or the manager doesn't really like them or a customer complained so we had to move them' (Jackie, dance manager, corporate club, southern city). High earners were more likely to be protected from dismissal than others who generated less revenue for the club.

Instead of hierarchical open control, other managers preferred styles of management based on an ethos of teamwork, as they felt that the well-being and attitude of the dancers was the route to a successful business. A female manager describes her approach to recruitment, where individuals were given a chance to try out the work before they committed:

> Basically, I ask the questions over the phone … and when they're ready they can come in. I tell them about the floor fees, how much it is, take them around the club, make sure that they're comfortable. And basically they work that night and if they feel comfortable enough then they can come again. But if not, you know, they're not obliged. Eventually if she continues to stay we'll ask her to go on the pole. We don't ask them to go on the pole until they're ready.
>
> (Jodie, assistant club manager, northern town)

Still, even with these forms of management with a human face, many noted how successful businesses operated by 'keeping the girls onside' and appealing to the notion of camaraderie and solidarity amongst 'the girls':

> My girls, because they've been with me a long time and I do try and treat them properly, they police it [the club] for me. They will tell me if a girl's being a bit naughty or stuffing money in her boot and not declaring how much she earns and all that sort of stuff. So I like to know my girls.
>
> (Jackie, dance manager, corporate club, southern city)

> Well, on a personal level with the girls we tend to know a bit more about their backgrounds and stuff, you know. You have like a little friendship as well, when you're a female as well. For the girls, to confide in a female – especially when it comes to like personal problems, like they need some scissors for their Tampax string and stuff.
>
> (Jodie, assistant club manager, northern town)

These insights both from female managers who had specific roles to organise dancers demonstrate how personal relationships and from the 'friendlier face' of management are used to carry out strategies of surveillance and to control the dancers.

Regulating sexual bodies not working bodies

It appears that the UK sexual entertainment licensing processes up to 2009 and continuing in many jurisdictions even after SEV licensing was adopted, regulated the body parts and sexuality of dancers in licensing law whilst their bodies as workers were ignored. Reflecting Jackson's (2011) sociological analysis of norms in the strip club legislation in Las Vegas, Nevada, we note that in relation to dancers in the UK the regulation of dancers has been overwhelming about their nakedness. As the UK licenses non-contact striptease (not the American-style lap dancing), the majority of licensing policies include significant details on the type of contact that is forbidden. A significant amount of the law is dedicated to setting detailed parameters of the performance and the ways in which dancers can use and display their bodies and interact with others.

Physical contact between customers and dancers, or dancers and dancers was totally banned in a number of localities: 'There shall be no physical contact between the performers and customers before, during or after the performance' (East Cheshire). The majority of policies recognised that some contact needed to be made by dancers when meeting and greeting customers, but were clear what was overstepping the regulatory mark. Bristol's policy was typical in stating the dancer should not 'kiss, stroke, fondle, caress or embrace any customer'. Often the policies subtract any normal physical interactions between two people in a social setting, with attempts to set the scene as sterile and non-sexual as possible.

The focus in regulation is on the body parts of the female labourer – although policies are written as gender neutral, in effect they are directed at female bodies. Women's sexuality is regulated through specific licensing conditions that disallow parts of the body to be shown and certain sexualised acts to be performed. Full nudity is controlled, so naked bodies can only appear in certain zones in the venue (for instance, on the stage or in the booths). Performers are expected to be clothed unless there are performing a private dance or stage show. In a few jurisdictions, only topless striptease was allowed: 'Full nudity is not permitted. Performers and employees must at all times wear at least a G-string or similar clothing covering the genitalia' (Blackpool). It was common that licensing criteria included a ban on dancers touching themselves during performances, touching others and being touched by customers: 'Performers must not when performing, intentionally touch the genitals or breasts of another dancer or to knowingly permit another dancer to intentionally touch their genitals or breasts' (Bournemouth). In law the body of the dancer is owned by the state as she plies her naked performance for money, taking care not to touch herself, engage with her own body or use her body parts as she fits to create the required fantasy, authenticity, or simply be herself.

The prescription of interactions between customers and dancers made by some policies indicates the level of regulatory control over the encounter: 'There shall be no physical participation between performers or any member of the audience and any performer (other than a normal socially acceptable greeting such as a handshake, light kiss on the cheek or placing of a hand on a shoulder or waist' (Lincoln). Other policies were extremely detailed in stating which activities were not allowed beyond meeting and greeting and the exchange of money. For instance Leicester includes a range of prohibitions: no sex toys, no audience participation, no mixed gender performance, no photography, no simulation of sex acts or masturbation, and no straddling customers. The underlining concerns here in this strict regulation of sexual bodies, sexual interactions and sexualised entertainment is the desire to ensure prostitution does not take place in a licensed premise. It is not possible to police the detailed restrictions of the female body, as this would mean that each individual interaction between the dancer and the customer is monitored. It also ignores the realities of human interactions which involved physical (not necessarily sexual) interactions when in a social environment.

Ultimately there is no autonomy given to the dancer (at least not formally), and the unrealistic extent to which the female body is regulated shows the extreme focus of the licensing concerns on controlling her body and not on making the working environment safer or a fair working space.

In the United States, as Jackson (2011) points out, this regulation of female sexuality is oppressive as venues where alcohol is on sale have a ban on total nudity, resulting in only topless stripping. Frank (2002) and Liepe-Levinson (2002) go further and claim that the strip club regulation reifies the good girl/bad girl dichotomy which penalises the bad girl image both legally (by legislating against nudity/acts) and economically (by not allowing women to earn money from their bodies as they see fit). This subtext to the law frames acceptable and unacceptable forms of sexuality in UK licensing. Concerns with the visibility of female sexuality mean that licensing conditions have strict rules on advertising stripping, and ensuring no signage suggests female sexuality (for instance, no silhouettes of the female form can be used in advertising or signage of strip venue). Concerns over 'out of control' female sexuality are bound up in moral panics over connections between strip clubs and trafficking and prostitution. The focus on controlling female sexuality within an inch of a pubic hair, touch of the hand or pucker of the lips reduces the performer to body parts and commercial sexuality, ignoring her body as a worker. Our conclusions are concerned with the more direct ways that dancers and their labour have been missed out of the licensing and regulation process as the state is more concerned with controlling her sexual body than considering her employment and working rights.

Regulating work?

In this chapter thus far we have described in depth the ways in which clubs are regulated by enforcement officials. To a lesser extent, if at all, do the needs and everyday work issues of dancers feature in the formal regulation of strip venues? This is partly due to the absence of an official organisation which held any remit for the welfare and working conditions of dancers other than the very basic standards of a workplace. There appears to be a split in enforcement responsibilities between licensing officials and the health and safety authorities. This leaves dancers' general safety and well-being potentially falling into an area which belongs to no particular agency. Priority for licensing enforcers tended to be related to compliance with licence conditions which are primarily concerned with minimising public disorder and nuisance and preventing forms of crime such as prostitution. At the time of the research, there was no scope for licensing conditions to consider dancer welfare and working conditions and these were not considered at all in the routine scrutiny process as they were considered beyond the concern of the licensing process. Seldom in the interviews with licensing officers was the issue of dancer welfare raised or commented on as it simply was not in their remit.

Health and safety officers had the least scrutiny powers (they did not do unannounced visits), yet were the only officials who tended to consider the dancers safety and well-being directly. Some health and safety officers felt standards could be improved for dancers. Suggestions included: safe and secure changing areas, washing facilities, lockers for valuables, somewhere to rest between dances, facilities for making food and drinks. The safety of dancers was considered and discussed most by health and safety enforcers as they usually quiz managers about policies for leaving work at the end of a shift for instance. Yet still, they were mainly concerned with the basic standards of a building being fit for public and employee use. There was only one comment that considered worker safety:

> I think things like slips and trips particularly if they're using water as part of their act on the dance floor or baby oil and that kind of thing on the, on the poles for doing pole dancing and that kind of thing.
>
> (Veronica, health and safety officer, northern city council)

Health and safety enforcers also considered bad practice to be associated with welfare of staff and dancers, and one licensing officer mentioned the poor back-stage areas and changing rooms she had witnessed and raised this as evidence of poor practice:

> We've recently had an issue with a lap dancing venue where the health and safety team came on board, where there was an allegation of slips and trips hazards. And also the heating system was too cold at night for the workers. There was also a suggestion that the number of hours the dancers were having to work was excessive and inflexible. So there were a number of considerations there and that was basically principally the health and safety team.
>
> (Adam, principal licensing officer, northern city council)

Others were concerned with how the non-touch condition is enforced:

> Although the clubs, or mostly specify, well, all the ones I've been to, specify on the websites no touching and quite strict rules but how it's enforced. You know, when money's involved, how do they enforce that?
>
> (Marie, environmental health officer and inspector of
> health and safety, northern city council)

Health and safety inspectors considered risks to dancers safety as assaults in the club, unwanted touching in the booth areas of the clubs, safety in getting home after a shift, and the risk of slipping and tripping on the dance floor and pole safety. General issues relevant for all workers were also noted; the frequency of breaks and the club temperature were welfare issues under the remit of health and safety. However, health and safety officers varied in how they saw their roles in relation to addressing safety concerns as there was a lack of clarity over whether they had the powers to enforce change. They noted some powers in relation to addressing risks, but one noted that these were not an enforcement issue, more one of good practice.

With the role of the dancer not appearing in official surveillance or scrutiny processes other than where sexuality is concerned, the operations and organisation of the club remain unchecked when it comes to treating dancers fairly. This chapter has noted the varying ways in which dancers are managed: some with care and respect, others as mere means to a profit-making end, where 'control' and 'order' is paramount. It is in these conditions, where the treatment of dancers is either ignored, unconsidered or unscrutinised, that exploitation is enabled to flourish.

Writing dancers welfare into policy

As a result of an impact and dissemination project (Sanders and Campbell 2012), funded by the Economic and Social Research Council (ESJ000035/1) as a follow-on project to the original research reported in this book, work has been done with key stakeholders (the Institute of Licensing and Licensing Committees) to make changes to how some Sexual Entertainment Venue (SEV) policies consider the working conditions of dancers. The original research project resulted in the following policy recommendations for the licensing of SEVs:

*   Clubs should provide access to adequate changing and kitchen facilities, requiring modifications to heating and air conditioning systems.
*   Fining should be banned as a form of discipline.
*   Receipts should be provided for fines, fees and commission.
*   Owners should be compelled to submit their codes of conduct to the local authority.
*   Conditions should ensure that performers who are sick or have a domestic emergency *are not made subject to unfair punitive financial penalties.*
*   Limits should be set on the number of dancers per capacity of clubs (to control competition).
*   Tighter regulation on the type of private booths to achieve privacy and security; including fitting panic buttons in booths.
*   Clubs to have a policy on dancer safety when leaving clubs.

As a result of a year of intensive work with licensing officers and licensing committees, dancer welfare and safety are now (to varying degrees) written into (a minimum of) twenty-five SEV policies in England and Wales. These conditions now range from banning fining and closed-off private booths, to improving physical conditions and facilities for dancers. This has been achieved through direct work with the Institute of Licensing, delivering presentations and workshops to licensing practitioners and providing training to licensing committees across England and Wales. We can demonstrate this by tracking how SEVs directly include our recommendations. The main examples are:

*   The introduction of a welfare pack for dancers which must include: fining policy; pricing policy; code of conduct; details of trade union representation; details of insurance; details of how to report a crime (Leeds). Other councils now require policies on dancer welfare (Camden, Islington, Wirral and Manchester).

Figure 7.2 Closed-off booths where private dances take place. Photograph by Liz Lock

- Tighter regulation on management and type of private booths. For instance, Manchester requires panic buttons, clear sight line for security, no enclosure; Brighton and Hove include security must have visibility, no curtain or barrier across entrance; Leeds states there must be direct supervision; Maidstone includes a condition of panic alarms; Leicester includes the monitoring of booths by security staff or CCTV; Islington asks for CCTV in all booths; Westminster now bans the use of private booths where supervision is inadequate; and Camden has banned booths outright.
- Clubs are required to clearly display council rules in a number of places in the club, in addition to codes of conduct for customers (Birmingham, Nottingham, Durham, Basildon, Leeds, Wigan, Cheshire East, Cornwall, Blackpool, Hillingdon, Leicester).
- Owners are required to submit their codes of conduct on house fees, commission and fining to the licensing authority (Leeds, Blackpool, Camden, Cheshire East, Cornwall, Hillingdon, Nottingham).

- Owners require council permission to change codes of conduct (Nottingham, Camden, Islington).
- Owners are required to provide receipts for fines, fees and commission (Birmingham) and some councils (Leeds) require a register of fines to be kept.
- Blackpool is the only council that includes a condition that ensures that performers who are sick or have a domestic emergency *are not made* subject to unfair punitive financial penalties.
- Camden has outright banned fining as a form of discipline.
- Minimum standards on physical conditions and facilities such as requiring clubs to provide access to adequate, secure, private changing and smoking areas (Blackpool, Bristol, Camden, Leicester, Leeds, Sheffield, Nottingham, Manchester, Maidstone, Wigan), requiring adequate heating (Wigan) and air conditioning systems (Blackpool) and provision of free water (Camden).
- Clubs must have a policy on dancers safety when leaving/arriving at the venue and/or arrangements for accompaniment/secure transport (Manchester, Brighton and Hove, Bournemouth, Cornwall, Islington, Leicester, Westminster, Newcastle, Sheffield, Nottingham, Durham, Basildon, Maidstone, Blackpool, Watford).
- In one case (Blackpool) clubs are required to limit the number of dancers per night in response to our recommendations.

Conclusion

The management of clubs has been significantly influenced by the processes of regulation set out by local authority licensing conditions. Licensing in relation to most of the night-time economy is mainly concerned with preventing and containing disorder and nuisance, and minimising the impact of strip clubs on the surrounding community. To deflect concerns about the 'riskiness' of the venues, clubs have mostly responded with strategies of 'professionalism' through formal styles of management and policies and procedures which mimic those of ordinary businesses. The economic mainstreaming of strip venues, particularly those in the larger UK cities, have encouraged a 'corporatisation' which acts both to attract corporate customers and to boost their cultural status as organised and legitimate night-time business. Strip clubs, particularly those who are part of franchises or chains, often appear to be compliant with the standard conditions of the licence and act quickly to make changes at the request of enforcement officers. Yet our research and analysis demonstrates that it is the internal operations and management that control the dancers' labour. It is in the modes of surveillance and strategies to control dancers through 'friendly faces' or authoritarian styles of management that dancers are often subject to unfair and exploitative treatment.

As standard, dancers' welfare and safety as part of their working conditions have historically not been considered in the licensing conditions and process as concerns relating to sexuality, prostitution and crime have taken precedence. Dancers as workers have been absent from policy, but instead their sexual bodies have been regulated as a response to fears about prostitution and other organised crimes. As a direct result of research findings that have been considered in relation to concrete and tangible recommendations for policy, dancers' welfare has now been written into some SEV policies in England and Wales. While the practical recommendations we suggested can only go a small way to reducing dancer exploitation and do not change the stringent management styles of businesses, the changes are nevertheless in the interest of dancers. We have demonstrated here that licensing committees are open to change, but they can only create evidence-based policy if they are aware of the (methodologically robust and ethical) evidence. Change lies within the licensing process rather than outside a regulatory framework. But it is within these confined processes of democracy and policy decision making that dancers (and other sex workers) are often silenced (see Sanders forthcoming).

The interesting twist in the politics of the stripping wars is that the anti-lap dancing lobby that called for the reclassification and the tighter regulation of strip venues by local authority has in effect laid open the policy-making process so that strip venues can be regulated properly in relation to dancer welfare and conditions. Thinking entirely of the concerns and issues that residents and the broader community have, Object (2008) campaigned for increasing powers at a local government level to control strip clubs. In effect, rather than have any dramatic influence on the number of SEVs and certainly not 'closing down' the industry, the anti-lap dancing lobbyists have provided a new licensing framework and the regulatory terrain for increased licensing conditions that can favour and improve clubs for dancers to work in. Attempts to shut down the industry have in fact provided mechanisms whereby the industry may be forced to improve standards, eliminate bad practice, and address dancers' working rights.

References

Bernstein, E. (2007) Sex work for the middle classes, *Sexualities* 10 (4): 473–88.

Bradley, M. (2008) Selling sex in the new millenium: thinking about changes in adult entertainment and dancers' lives, *Sociology Compass* 2 (2): 503–18.

Brents, B. and Sanders, T. (2010) The mainstreaming of the sex industry: economic inclusion and social ambivalence, *Journal of Law and Society* 37 (1): 40–60.

Chatterton, P. (2002) Governing nightlife: profit, fun and (dis)order in the contemporary city, *Entertainment Law* 1 (1): 23–49.

Colosi, R. (2010) *Dirty Dancing. An Ethnography of Lap-Dancing*, Cullompton, Devon: Willan.

Frank, K. (2002) *G-Strings and Sympathy: Strip Club Regulars and Male Desire*, London: Duke University Press.

Jackson, C. (2011) Revealing contemporary constructions of femininity: expression and sexuality of strip club regulation, *Sexualities* 14 (3): 354–69.

Liepe-Levinson, K. (2002) *Strip Show: Performances of Gender and Desire*, New York: Routledge.

Object (2008) *Stripping the Illusion: Countering Lap Dancing Industry Claims*. Online: www.object.org.uk/index.php?option=com_content&view=article&id=1&Itemid=11 (accessed 13 August 2013).

Price, K. (2008) Keeping the dancers in check: the gendered organization of stripping work in the lion's den, *Gender & Society* 22 (3): 367–89.

Roberts, R., Jones, A. and Sanders, T. (2013) Students and sex work in the uk: providers and purchasers, *Sex Education: Sexuality, Society and Learning* 13 (3): 349–63.

Sanders, T. (forthcoming) Regulating strip-based entertainment: sexual entertainment venue policy and the ex/inclusion of dancers' perspectives and needs, *Social Policy and Society*.

Sanders, T. and Campbell, R. (2012) *Sexual Entertainment Venues: Regulating Working Conditions*, Economic and Social Research Council (ESJ000035/1).

Sanders, T. and Campbell, R. (2013) Sexual entertainment venue policies: analysing trends, conditions and improvements in dancer welfare and safety, *Journal of Licensing* 2 (3).

Sanders, T. and Hardy, K. (2014) Students selling sex: marketisation, higher education and consumption, *British Journal of Sociology of Education*.

8 Speaking back

The feminist and class politics of stripping

Introduction

As the opening of this book describes, stripping and 'lap dancing' clubs have become highly politicised, as a key site for the contestation not only of the clubs themselves but also of wider issues of gender and women's rights at the front lines of the feminist civil war over issues of sex and sexuality (cf. Dworkin 1989: Mackinnon 1989; Segal and McIntosh 1992; Shrage 1994, 2005). The debates and activism that have emerged around strip clubs in the UK are, in many ways, simply the latest incarnation of the long-running debates within the feminist movement around pornography and 'prostitution', emergent in the 1970s and definitive of the fault lines in the feminist movement ever since.

As part of what has been seen as a new ascendency of feminism in the UK (Dean 2012; Thorpe 2013), characterised by the emergence of new feminist organisations and the publication of a tranche of popular feminist books, the campaign group Object came to make a hegemonic claim as being *the* feminist perspective and organisation active in politics around strip clubs. Through the course of these debates, in which particular media-friendly feminist activists have been rendered 'celebrity' voices, dancers' voices have been systematically obscured or silenced, albeit offering space for 'survivor' stories emanating from ex-dancers who condemn the industry (see, for example, the collaboration between Hayashi Danns and Object 2011). The mundane experiences of current dancers remain concealed from view. As such, it has not been clear how dancers feel about these debates or their identifications and (dis)associations with feminism and the politics around strip clubs. As such, in this chapter we explore dancers' feelings about the politics of stripping, feminism and how they locate themselves and their labour within these debates. We juxtapose the arguments that have dominated the popular press and parts of the mainstream liberal and radical feminist activism with dancers' own perspectives and the alternative feminist politics proposed by dancers themselves, alternative feminist groups and sex workers' organisations.

We argue that the focus on a particular type of gender equality by anti-lap dancing feminists lacks a class and intersectional analysis and in doing so has constituted some women as deserving of rights, safety and protection, while rendering erotic dancers as undeserving of similar privileges. More seriously, we assert that this lack of class analysis and recognition of the material conditions of dancers' lives as workers has failed to improve working conditions in strip clubs and even served to disempower dancers in their workplaces and concentrate power in the hands of their employers. We use the case study of Sexual Entertainment Venue licensing in the borough of Hackney, London, to explore the ways in which these politics have played out in practice, demonstrating that beyond the purported (and simplistic) gender politics of Object and others, there are much wider political issues at play. These include the elision of class differences between women, the operationalisation of power through legalistic appeals to the state, and the role of such politics in gentri-fication and the new forms of urban revanchism which seek to remove undesirable people and places and remake the city as a space of middle-class consumption.

Contrasting with claims that the new legislation would improve conditions for women in the stripping industry, we note that, thus far, legislation has brought lit-tle change for workers and instead outline the ways in which dancers themselves articulate that their conditions could be improved. Finally, we point to emergent organising practices between feminists and dancers and argue that their analyses of stripping work, which take into account the wider political economy which is productive of the expansion of the strip industry, offer green shoots in struggles for improving dancers' lives, as women, workers and people.

Objecting to Object

Object's campaign 'Stripping the Illusion', launched in 2008, aimed to re-license strip clubs as distinct from other venues in the night-time economy. They claimed that 'lap dancing clubs normalise the sexual objectification of women, create "no go" areas for women and are a form of commercial sexual exploitation'.[1] The group, which has full-time paid activists and volunteers, works on multiple issues around the issue of sexual objectification including a campaign to end 'demand' for sexual labour.[2] While others have empirically tested the notion that clubs threaten women's safety in public space, finding that a small minority considered clubs a public nui-sance on any terms (Hubbard and Colosi 2013), we have problematised a simplistic notion of 'objectification' in encounters in the strip club (see further Chapter 6) and demonstrated that – contrary to emphasis on 'demand' – much of the expansion of the stripping industry is founded on a labour supply produced by wider conditions of marketised education, lack of well-paid flexible work, and the poor conditions and low pay found in the unskilled service sector (as discussed in Chapter 5).

Object have been a vocal and powerful actor in the debates around legislative change and yet dancers have rarely been offered the opportunity to 'speak back'. During the 'Stripping the Illusion' campaign, dancers in Hackney offered Object the opportunity to meet to discuss their position:

> Initially, we naively just thought that they'd misunderstood. We just thought 'Oh, they've just got everything wrong. When they meet us they'll see.' How naïve this all seems now.
>
> (Edie, 33, white British)

of the movement. How dare you tell me what I can and what I can't do with my body?

(Faith, 34, white British)

Katy (25, white British) emphasised a similarly sexual libertarian position: 'I just think people take things too seriously. A naked body is the most natural thing in the world.' Some, however, articulated an alternative gendered analysis of the campaign to specifically target women's nude entertainment:

It's a very sexist thing they're doing, because they're dissuading women from doing a job they might want to, why? Because we're not good enough or something? Or what? … It's basically saying to women, you can't do this certain job because we don't think it's good enough. We think by doing it, you're making yourself into some sort of beaten housewife.

(Dalia, 20, white British)

Dalia's comparison of dancers with 'housewives' is instructive in that she chooses to raise the identity of a housewife (albeit one suffering domestic violence) as an oppressed identity, in opposition to – in her eyes – the relatively more emancipated dancer. Bella similarly relativised dancing in comparison to other parts of the waged economy, finding it more favourable:

It's not as if I'm being dragged here … even girls that are foreign who come into the country and want to work and earn some money, it's not a bad job. It's easy. The only thing that's hard is talking to people you don't like. That's the hard thing about it. If you cared about taking your clothes off, you wouldn't do it.

(Bella, 26, white British)

Contrary to dancers' own articulations of their work, explained in terms of enjoyment, strategic use and a relativisation of the labour of stripping compared to alternative forms of work (Chapter 5), Sian, who had been involved in activism against strip clubs in the north of England, said that she suspected that:

people with certain sort of experiences in their past would be over represented … I don't have any evidence to back this up, but I would suspect that there would be … people who had had childhood sort of sexual abuse or had been valued for being pretty or decorative as in their earlier lives would be over-represented in that job.

This was not reflected in our findings, which demonstrated acutely that working in dancing was a pragmatic decision about where's women's labour could be sold for the most money and which would offer the most flexibility (Chapter 4). Such narratives of 'false consciousness' are commonly used amongst those who argue for the closure of strip clubs and the abolition of other parts of the sex industry. Many of these anti-lap dancing activists dismiss the voices of those currently working in the industry on the basis that they perform deep acting and self-delusion in order to 'survive' the work:

> I worry about talking to them about it and it might be difficult for them, for the reasons I've said, because they have to tell themselves that they're enjoying it, and some of them they have to enjoy it otherwise they couldn't get through the day.
>
> (Sian, anti-lap dancing activist)

Faith had direct experience of this, during a radio interview with an objector, in which the other guest 'actually said "well maybe you were abused by your father my dear and you blanked it out"'. The violence of such narratives was frequently cited by dancers as a dark irony, considering that such arguments were frequently vouched in the name of combating violence against women. These claims were experienced by dancers as deeply degrading as claims of false consciousness act as a denial of personhood: the ability to think or act with autonomy (Cornell 1995). Suzanna argued that the fetishisation of sex work and the 'pornographic' (Faith) tone of these narratives 'causes us, as workers, to feel creeped out and abused'. They further highlighted the use of such discourses as key mechanisms for silencing dancers and invalidating any analyses and articulations of their own experiences:

> Their justification for not speaking to dancers and not listening to us because no – nothing that comes out of our mouths can be trusted because we're in this false consciousness, dream world. And that is so offensive.
>
> (Faith, 34, white British)

Faith reported attending a House of Commons meeting on the Policing and Crime Bill with another dancer, after which her and a colleague 'felt almost physically abused as a result of hearing all this crap, that we were literally speechless … its upsetting and its angering' being spoken about by 'people who know so little about you' (Faith). Suzanna articulated such narratives as a 'chronically violent tactic', which are experienced by the dancers as an intense form of symbolic and corporeal violence.

Dancers often articulated sophisticated critiques of the types of terms that anti-lap dancing activists used, including both 'feminism'. In addition to questioning how such approaches could be considered 'feminist', a number of women dis-identified from feminism. When asked if she thought of herself as a feminist, Faith replied:

> I wouldn't use that term, no. I mean I actually don't know a huge amount about – it's something I never really studied at college or anything like that so I don't know enough about it. I would want to say no compared to the people who do identify themselves as feminists, who spout all this crap.
>
> (Faith, 34, white British)

Despite this dis-affiliation from 'feminism' by some dancers, many of the dancers did identify as feminists and all of them described nuanced differences between multiple forms of feminism. Emma said 'I would definitely identify as a feminist, but I'm much more Camille Paglia[3] than Object' and in responding to the question of whether she was a feminist, Edie said:

> The label [feminist] has become so tarnished and hijacked by Mary White-house-style morality campaigners. As a woman of course, you want to be treated equally and given equal opportunities, but it's become so distracted and so dragged into the mud by these crazy groups. You want to be like, well yeah, I'm a feminist, but not that kind!
>
> (Edie, 33, white British)

As Edie, Emma and others indicate, there is not only one feminist politics of stripping. Dancers posited their own versions of feminism, often reflecting 'sex positive' feminism:

> Another thing is that it's denying a part of who you are. You're allowed to have a job now as a woman, you're allowed to earn money, you're allowed to own property, but are you allowed to be sexual as well? Do you have to be Miss Prim? Or a slut? We have to get beyond this issue about sexuality and sexual expression. It's fun doing a sexy dance on stage, it is fun to perform. And you do start to understand yourself better as well.
>
> (Emma, 31, Belgian)

Ava Caradonna, the collective identity of members of x:talk, a sex workers' rights collective, which includes many dancers, for example, identifies as 'an activist, prostitute, migrant, student, feminist, stripper, radical, actress, porn star, film maker, English teacher'.[4] The feminism of Ava Caradonna therefore emphasises the multiple social categories that women inhabit, emphasising the intersecting nature of individuals' positions – for example, within the labour market and class hierarchies – as well as their relationship to immigration controls and racial hierarchies.

While few dancers voiced an overarching critique of the structural conditions which shaped their work, many did point to material reasons why women danced (namely the need to earn a wage in order to survive). They therefore asserted that undermining the ability to earn money in this sector therefore represented an attack on women's autonomy and financial independence and questioned how this could be construed as a feminist act:

> They're then preventing us earning money in that way … I mean god, there's a lot of women that rely on this kind of money; for example there's … women … [who] want to see their kids okay. They want to bring them up. But at the same time they need to earn money. They don't have the time or the education to like – to go out and do other kind of jobs.
>
> (Matilda, 24, white British)

As Matilda points out, this had a particularly strong effect on working-class women for whom education is less available and for whom the alternative labour options would not provide sufficient time to undertake their (unpaid) responsibilities for social reproduction.

The politics of SEV licensing: the case of Hackney

Hackney, a borough in East London, offers an interesting case in terms of the ways in which struggles over SEV licensing have played out. The geography of this borough is notable in that it borders the City of London, home to the heart of global finance capitalism and yet is a traditionally working-class borough, with large African-Caribbean and other migrant populations (Seymour 2009). In many ways, Hackney represents an archetypal microcosm of the wider 'hourglass' economy of London, with sharply polarised working conditions at either end of the labour market with highly paid and skilled occupations at one end and 'poorly paid and unskilled "servicing" jobs at the bottom end' (McDowell 2001: 455; Sassen 1991).

In 2003, Hackney was a 'mixed area and one in which the middle class have not succeeded in exerting their hegemony' (Butler 2002: no page). In the decade since 2003, while remaining mixed, intensified gentrification in Hackney has seen areas such as Shoreditch (in addition to Columbia Road or Broadway Market) become increasingly dominated by middle-class consumption (Seymour 2009). This change is evident in the emergence of a dense concentration of expensive bars, cafes, restaurants, health food stores and boutique shops, accompanied by rocketing commercial and residential property prices. Shoreditch, a neighbourhood in the southern part of the borough that directly borders on to Liverpool Street and the City of London, has become an important space of night-life consumption in the city, associated with, but not limited to, city workers and workers from the growth industries such as media, design and advertising, industries populated by young upwardly mobile professionals. As such, Shoreditch has been subject to a process of intense gentrification whereby young middle-class professionals have transformed the residential and commercial geography of the neighbourhood by buying up the housing stock and driving the proliferation of venues for middle-class consumption, with both processes 'lubricating the revalorisation of the inner city' (Lees 2000: 392).

Surrounded by this high density of night-time drinking venues in Shoreditch are four strip clubs and one sex shop. Many of the clubs have been in business for over thirty years and constitute a somewhat traditional part of the fabric of the area. They are spatially concentrated on one road within about a quarter of mile at the south end of the borough. Most are 'strip pubs' rather than clubs, with some offering only stage dancing and others offering a combination of stage and private dancing (see Chapter 3). This juxtaposition between spaces of respectable or 'tasteful' bourgeois consumption and working-class workplaces can be understood as a local geographical expression of London's polarised hourglass economy.

In September 2010, Hackney Borough Council launched a consultation on their draft Sexual Establishment Venue Licensing policy, following the adoption of the Local Government (Miscellaneous Provisions) Act 1982 as part of the Policing and Crime Act 2009. The draft document proposed a measure that would determine that the appropriate number of clubs in the borough as equal to zero (what has colloquially been known as the 'nil policy'). It was estimated that this could lead to a loss of 300 jobs, not just limited to dancers but also including door and bar staff and others such as cleaners who worked in the venues (GMB press release). The consultation was seen by dancers and club owners, as well as many members of the community including shop owners and a local vicar, as mounting to an attack on established members of the community. The GMB branch of the International Union of Sex Workers (IUSW), who represent workers across the sex industry, stated that 'this is a sexist proposal. There is a huge hypocrisy of the female run, owned and staffed venues being targeted but the gay sex encounters venues in Shoreditch being exempt and unaffected by the "nil" policy' (GMB Press Release, 7 December 2010). Reverend Paul Turp, vicar from Shoreditch Church, voiced his opposition to the 'nil policy' proposal on the grounds that it would make conditions less safe for dancers and that existing venues were safe and well run. He condemned the proposal as undermining safety and security for dancers, vilifying the nil policy as a 'wretched mistake' (Osborne 2011).

The council stated that when considering applications, they would seek to balance 'the conflicting needs of commercial interests, patrons, employees, residents and communities'.[5] While the chief officer of police for Hackney was consulted, along with owners or managers, 'regulatory authorities such as the fire authority, community safety and child protection' and 'resident associations and trade associations', no consultation took place with dancers in the venues. Confronted with the threat of closure of their workplaces and without inclusion in the consultation or a clear line of communication with the council, dancers started to self-organise:

> The first thing we heard of it, the rumour mill got going and we heard that they're going to shut all the clubs in the borough. So we started looking up and reading about it. I was more educated and had a better grasp of English than some of the other dancers, so they asked me to look over some of the papers. There were discussion groups and we got together and talked about it and there were other LGBT groups. There was a lot of collaboration between girls in all the clubs, it was actually really great, it brought people together like that.
>
> (Emma, 31, Belgian)

Many of the dancers who were key to organising opposition to the nil policy were 'professionals' (see Chapter 5) and dancers who preferred the stage shows and culture of the East End pubs. Many of them had worked in the Hackney strip clubs for over a decade, meaning they had nascent networks which they were able to mobilise:

We had emails going around between us, there's quite a network because people move between clubs, so if you've already worked there for quite a few years, you already know a lot of people, so it was already quite established, a bit of a network. So the ones of us who had worked there long enough, the ones who had a stake in it, we really were primary stakeholders in this issue.

(Emma, 31, Belgian)

In addition to online petitions and submissions to the consultation, on 10 December the IUSW GMB branch and recently formed Hackney Dancers' Alliance – a group of strippers and dancers who had formed a network – held a demonstration outside Hackney City Hall. In addition, they posted blogs and made a video entitled 'Hands Off', available on YouTube.[6]

Nearly three thousand (2705) survey responses were received in response to the consultation, in addition to emails and letters (72), during the twelve-week period from September to December 2010. A majority (66 per cent) of the public who responded to the consultation voted against the proposal of a 'nil policy'. The council admitted that 'the outcome of the consultation showed that there was significant opposition to the proposal to apply the nil policy to existing premises', as consultees alluded to premises being 'long standing, well run and of little concern to their locality'.[7] Despite this resistance to the implementation of a 'nil' policy, it was all the same adopted by the council, albeit with an amendment so that while existing premises were not required to close, no further licenses would be issued.

Figure 8.1 Hackney Dancers' Alliance protest over possible closure of their workplace. Photograph by Charlie Pycraft/ YDPR.co.uk

her right to access the upper echelons of her career path appears in stark contrast to the ability of the stripper to earn her income in the strip club.

This juxtaposition of boardroom versus the strip club reflects the prioritisation of the needs and values of professional women over women dancing in the clubs in the discourses of anti-lap dancing campaigners. The strategy of simply closing down strip clubs has the effect of kicking away the ladder for dancers who are using stripping as one of few ways to pay for an education (for a discussion see Chapter 4) or of condemning women to work in the low-paid service jobs, in which sexual harassment is widely noted by customers, managers and co-workers alike (Hughes and Tadic 1998). In rendering strip clubs uniquely sexist sites of harassment and sexism, such an approach obscures the common sexism and harassment faced by women across the labour market and its pervasive prevalence in the service sector, in which female workers are routinely sexualised (Adkins 1995; Williams 2003).

The attempt to remove strip clubs as part of the historical fabric of Shoreditch can be understood as the logical end point of gentrification, as 'once this process of "gentrification" starts in a district it goes on rapidly until all or most of the original working class occupiers are displaced and the whole social character of the district is changed' (Glass 1964: xviii). It is notable that as these debates were occurring, raids on working premises in other sectors of the sex industry in East London intensified, with seventy raids in the five Olympic boroughs between January and August 2010 (Cacciottolo 2012; see also Peachey 2012). To put this in context, this equated to 1.16 raids or visits per London borough compared with fourteen per Olympic borough. This was combined with wider attempts to clear streets in the Olympic boroughs of street sex work (Peachey 2012).

Combined with crack downs on brothels and street sex work in conjunction with the Olympics, this use of licensing to control (and potentially remove) strip clubs in the areas can be understood as a revanchist strategy to transform East London by cleansing it of those elements that sully the middle-class landscape. In this context, Object's discourses and strategies for intervention provide the moral pretext for the repressive cleansing of sex workers' workplaces, creating a moral climate of outrage and *objection* in which state-led gentrification is legitimised. As such, Object and the state have formed an unlikely 'urban ruling class alliance' (Jessop 2002) to gentrify the East End by cleansing it of the visible signs of sex work, an illustrative example of the enactment of neo-liberal urban governance through (unaccountable) partnerships of governmental and non-governmental actors (Harvey 1989; Gillespie 2013).

Mitchell (2003) argues that the revanchist governance of urban space seeks to manage the urban environment as a 'landscape'. Importantly, the desired landscape is a 'place of comfort and relaxation, perhaps of leisurely consumption, unsullied by images of work, poverty, or social strife' (Mitchell 2003: 186). As such, Hackney is rendered as a place of leisure, catering to particular middle-class consumption values, rather than a site of work for women who make their livelihood in such places. In this case, the city is reclaimed as a space in which middle-class, suburban sensibilities are valued over the ability for women to earn a living. Yet by making a claim to universal 'gender equality', the competing interests *between* women are disguised and those of working sex workers are deprioritised.

Such 'revanchist' narratives construct men as the embodiment of threatening male sexuality and of strippers as undesirable subjects, placed in stark contrast to the ideal figure of the 'good' woman forced to walk past the strip club facades (many of which are unnotable as stripping venues due to licensing conditions). Revanchist discourses that justify the expulsion of undesirable subjects and activities from the inner-city landscape typically imply that these subjects and activities threaten the 'quality of life' of the community (Smith 1996: 225) Yet, as Gillespie (2013) points out 'of course, this rhetoric begs the question: "quality of life for whom?"' For those actors who wish to cleanse Hackney of its strip clubs, it is clear that their imagined community is one in which in strippers have no place. It is not clear how 'quality of life' may improve for women forced to work in the bottom half of the hourglass economy or lose access to a form of work (stripping) that they experience as less exploitative than the alternatives available to them, and cleansing the East End of London of visible signs of sex work of course does little to address the structural factors which shape the labour supply into stripping.

Improving the industry, suggestions for better practice

In addition to legitimising new licensing laws for the benefit of women in the 'community', Object make a secondary claim that the new SEV licensing they have advocated 'will better protect women who work in lap dancing clubs'.[11] When asked in 2013 about the changes that had taken place in the industry in the two years following the change in law, dancers reported that they had seen little change. Emma (31, Belgian) said, somewhat sardonically:

> We got a new shower. Huge changes. Definitely worth all that money they spent on the public consultation. Definitely money well spent. Nothing has changed. In terms of working conditions, nothing has changed.

In reality, licensing appears to have done little to improve conditions. This may be in part because improving conditions for dancers was, in fact, never the intention of the legislation, which was instead designed simply to limit and control the number of venues. The nod towards consideration for women dancing in strip clubs by both the council and by Object appears to be little more than an afterthought to defend against the charge that neither organisation cared about women working in strip venues.

In fact, some of the measures promoted by the campaign against stripping venues have actually had detrimental effects for dancers. Raising the cost of the licence fee was touted as an important step in reducing the number of clubs, but Una (29, Estonian) summarised the fears of many dancers, stating this carried the risk that 'if they put the licence fees up, they might raise our fees as well. Even if the government put it up, it doesn't help us.' There were other fears that the industry would become less, rather more, safe. Matilda (24, white British) said that although the industry did need 'a big change':

> what they're doing at the minute is changing it for the worse, because it's just going to push it underground, because there are more illegal clubs opening where they're run by people that we don't want them to be run by.

She pointed out that more openness about the clubs offered dancers more recourse to make demands on the council with regard to licensing fees and ask them to incorporate their interests in the licensing conditions. In particular, the introduction of 'nil policies' in places such as Hackney has served to concentrate power in the hands of the existing clubs. A small group of dancers wishing to open their own, independently run, co-operative venue have now found themselves in a position in which they are unable to get a licence and instead have to remain working in conditions of exploitation by club owners. The introduction of a nil policy in neighbouring Tower Hamlets also places this borough out of bounds for dancers seeking to assert their autonomy and escape conditions in which their surplus value is extracted by owners and managers.

Dancers themselves were highly articulate about the changes that they felt would improve conditions. This related to increasing the age at which women could start dancing to twenty-one, suggesting that this would both limit labour supply into the industry and ensure that women were more emotionally ready to take on the 'toll' (Barton 2006) of the industry and to try to ensure they were not using too much alcohol or recreational drugs while dancing. More simply, dancers spoke about changing the physical layout of the clubs. Katy advocated more security, more cameras and having booths that were not completely private, but that could be part of more general surveillance in the club. Panic buttons in booths were also advocated by a number of dancers.

In particular, however, dancers had clear views about changing the working conditions in which they laboured. Gabriela (32, Spanish/Venezuelan) compared the current state of the industry in the UK with what she had experienced in Australia where she was treated 'like a proper performer'. The clubs had facilities, including gyms and sunbeds, a kitchen to make a hot meal and individualised lockers with keys. Dancers were paid a wage and then they took commission from dancing, tying the clubs interests with dancers' income, rather than detaching it from it: '[the] way that it works is that they will take a percentage of your dancing, so if you make money, they make money' (Gabriela).

Fees in particular were cited as in need of regulation in order to ensure that dancers were not taking on the financial risk for the clubs. Similarly Ines (35, Spanish) argued that reducing the labour supply would also help to combat the 'race to the bottom' (see Chapter 4), as this is what made the industry so competitive and allowed people to undercut each other. Faith also argued that this would contest the disposability of the dancers, as dancers become recognised generators of value, rather than simply direct sources of it.

Ines argued that there needed to be a charter for clubs which was a 'syndicate for the whole stripping world'. This would regulate clubs at a different scale, meaning that not only did clubs have to adhere to local licensing conditions, which can create uneven geographies of regulation, but also there was standardisation of practice:

> Clubs would have to adhere to some kind of rules, the kinds of fees they charge. To introduce some kind of system whereby they pay tax for every single fee that they're charging, because they're not and that's how they get away with it. If they had to pay tax on everything, they wouldn't bother.
>
> (Ines, 35, Spanish)

Regulations on the number of women working on any one night was mentioned by multiple dancers. Matilda thought that fifteen to twenty was the maximum, while Ines thought that it should be proportional to the capacity of the club: 'so [if] the club can fit 300 guys, so the maximum number of girls is 30: 10 per cent' (Ines). In addition to fees, some felt that commission should reflect the level of custom that the club brought in.

Katy and Ines wanted stricter rules around touching, which she felt would stop the 'race to the bottom', which was a key process undermining standards (further discussed in Chapter 4). Matilda also reinforced this position:

> I'd say clubs really, really have to stick to the no soliciting, no extras. No – any of that; no touching – that really should not be allowed. I just think – I mean I don't know that it would work in every club, having the no – no contact rule. But no contact on the man's side and no girls doing any extras.
>
> (Matilda, 24, white British)

Further, many dancers argued that no touching rules should not be enforced through fines, but through more standard labour practices of suspension or dismissal.

A reduction of the number of venues and also labour supply was cited as a mechanism for reducing competition between dancers. 'Professional' dancers felt that reducing the level of labour supply and the number of venues would increase skill levels in the industry and reduce the 'deskilling' which had taken place, which had an important role in opening up the labour market. This would lead, Eerikka (36, Finnish) argued, 'to a better quality entertainment. The whole place, the whole thing would get a better name for itself.' Faith argued that increasing the skill level and the quality would also increase respect for dancers, both in their workplaces and more generally. It should be noted, however, that dancers were never supportive of their own venue being the one that was shut down and if we accept the argument that this work is an important source of economic freedom for women, the closure of venues would have discriminatory effects on who was able to access this work.

In addition to this, a number of dancers challenged the conditions of the 'myth of self-employment' (discussed in Chapter 5), as Matilda (24, white British) clearly stated 'they've got to choose one or the other. The girls are either self-employed or they're employed by the club.' She argued that if they wanted to control their labour, then they would have to pay them a wage and then they could also take commission on the dances, 'but if they just want us to be self employed, I'd say maybe [they'd have to] break up the shifts a bit, so like a girl can choose then her hours … cos I mean for me personally, I just think it's too long to do 8 till 6'. She continued:

> I think if they want to pay them a wage and then obviously they then get com-mission on dances as well. Which is only fair, then great. We will work the hours that you say we're going to work 'cos at least we're guaranteed some kind of money.

There was, however, ambivalence about securing conditions of employment that would involve a signed contract:

> Maybe it would be good to have a contract where you can't be dismissed so easily, but at the same time, a lot of the reason that we do this job is because we want to come and go.
>
> (Bella, 26, white British)

Cruz (2013) has pointed out that some sex worker activists have argued for further mainstreaming of sex work into the capitalist labour market, yet as Bella and other dancers have emphasised, the flexibility and at times – the liminal – nature of the work is its key attraction (see Chapter 5). However, the key question remains as to how working conditions can be improved while maintaining the autonomy that dancers desire (see Cruz 2013 for more).

While it should be noted that some licensing officials and councils are paying closer attention to evidence in shaping their licensing procedures (see Chapter 7), this was far from standard practice. Had dancers been consulted, the legisla-tion developed through the Policing and Crime Act and in the localised licensing conditions could have led to much clearer and more effective regulation of clubs in the interests of dancers, rather than simply regulating them from the outside, to protect women, the 'public' and 'community' outside the clubs. Dancers were very able to articulate the ways in which the industry needs improving, from the particular standpoint of the knowledge they had gained through their lived experi-ences. Yet, as dancers here have pointed out, their voices were not ones that were deemed appropriate to intervene in such debates.

Dancers cited examples of 'best practice', this included clubs which held man-datory staff meetings that increased democracy between dancers and manager and in which: 'you had to be there, because then you can actually get in and say your opinions and the girls can actually have a say in the way that the club is run' (Dalia, 20, white British). Faith and others cited a venue in the south of London which had moved from agency supplied labour to taking staff in-house by booking dancers directly through the club and reducing the fee, which Faith argued had a number of cumulative effects:

> The pub now books the girls themselves … they've reduced the fee to a fiver … [When it went] in-house suddenly a lot of the girls … were like, 'oh I'll go back there yeah' and 'cos the fee was reduced, suddenly everyone was like, 'I wanna work there', the pub therefore had their choice of girls, they could pick and choose, they've got the best girls there now, [and] the girls are happy.

As this fee paid for new promotion by the pub (such as a website rebranding) and improved safety conditions, dancers saw their money was not simply going into the manager's profit margins: 'we don't mind paying it and if you have a quiet shift you don't feel ripped off and so you're, you're still relatively happy' (Faith, 34, white British). She argued that this reversed the downward spiral and hostility between dancers and customers, and created a more amenable affective – as well as material – working environment.

Collective organisation

Collective self-organisation is key to improving the standards of any industry and is a particularly important starting point from within the sex industries (Cornell 1995).

Beyond the localised examples of collective organising evidenced in Hackney, formal collective organisation – particularly in the form of unions – was not widely mentioned by dancers as a solution to the contradictory experiences they faced and their dissatisfaction with certain aspects of their jobs, nor has it been a solution – to date – in practice. Faith recognised the value of trade union representation for offering a collective voice in order for dancers to contest their treatment as 'a disposable source of income'. Katy, Heidi and Nina also said that they would be likely to join a union, if approached. Nina said she thought it would offer a place to find advocacy and protection, as 'when you are treated unfairly there [would be] actually something you can do about it rather than just having to accept it'.

These dancers, however, represented a minority of dancers who felt that a formal trade union would be an appropriate mode of organisation for them. For Julia, the high level of labour supply meant that unionisation was not an appropriate option, as, 'if you're in a union and you're going to go on strike, especially in London, there's 40 … girls who're going to take your place quite happily'. Indeed, management have historically responded aggressively to unionisation campaigns in strip clubs (Chun 1999) (much like any industry) and Matilda thought that dancers would be concerned about antagonising management and owners:

> I think they'd worry about how it would affect how the club would then treat you … like what the effects would be on kind of the working relationship … I mean god, sometimes it's hard enough to kind of get along with management, but if they knew you were part of a union.

The temporariness and transitory nature that women understood as marking their engagement in the industry meant that many dancers dis-identified from their work in dancing and therefore had little interest in doing anything to change the industry. Chiara (22, white British) said that she would be unlikely to join a union as 'it's not something I want to do for the rest of my life and I don't think there are any other benefits I could reap from it'. Since it was largely only 'profession-als' who had occupational identification with the industry, most dancers' position somewhat reflected Chun's (1999: 245) assertion that 'an acceptance of unionism may represent a resignation to the sex industry, imbedding a sense of permanency and legitimacy in an occupation intended to be temporary'.

Two major unions accept dancers as members: the IUSW (International Union of Sex Workers) Adult Entertainment branch of the GMB and Equity, the actors' union. Yet many dancers disassociated from the IUSW, as a desire to avoid the whore stigma associated with the term 'sex work':

> When I was quite new with Union [IUSW] and I was telling all the dancers about it, as soon as I said Sex Workers, [they said] 'I'm not a sex worker, I'm not a prostitute', you know … so there was that fundamental problem.
>
> (Faith, 34, white British)

The idea of officially identifying as a dancer through affiliation also threatened some dancers' desire (or need) for discretion (see also Chun 1999). Even though it was possible to join the IUSW using a 'stage name' even that, Faith claimed, 'in reality … freaks people out'.

The erosion of collective labour practices and power of unions over the last forty years and the hatred articulated in the mass media towards unions, their members and actions means that dancers – much like many in the wider popula-tion – may be cynical of collective action. Heidi had never been approached and admitted that she didn't 'really understand what they are or what they do' and that she had heard of 'a little leaflet going around about the sex industry union, but I didn't really pay any attention'.

Despite brief organising successes in a small number of clubs including Club Crème in Bristol and the Majingos in Canary Wharf, these appear to have been short lived. Faith said that a year after the union recognition at the London club (Majingos), on consulting the women that worked there: 'they didn't even seem to know that the Union existed'. She asserted that she thought the two clubs had embraced unionisation cynically for public relations (PR) purposes, in order 'to ride on the back of the promotion, the publicity'. Finally, as in any labour-organis-ing drive, the fact that unions not having been able to win in the industry was also an issue: '[dancers] turn round to me and go, so what have they actually done for you, it's like well, nothing really' (Faith).

Beyond formal union organising, however, there have been a number of other organisations around stripping that do adopt analyses based not only on gender but also on complex intersections between race, migration policy, borders, class and capital. These alliances between feminists, lap dancers and feminist lap danc-ers such as the 'Red Umbrella Contingent' (Chapter 1) are made up of (amongst others) anti-capitalist collective Feminist Fightback, the sex workers' collective x:talk and Sex Workers Open University (SWOU). These organisations, which self-identify as feminist, have faced multiple instances of exclusion and discursive de-legitimation from other parts of the feminist movement. The Red Umbrella contingent emerged in response to aggression towards supporters of sex workers rights on the Reclaim the Night marches of 2006–08 and the rising exclusion of sex workers who identify as such in the wider feminist movement.[12] Sex workers and their allies reported being told they were unwelcome at the marches and some activists even faced physical violence. At a recent women's conference in Nottingham, sex workers from SWOU who argue for sex work to be understood as a form of wage labour were excluded from the event, with the event organisers citing issues of health and safety and capacity, despite having been implored to include organisations supporting decriminalisation in an open letter prior to the conference.[13]

Feminist activists arguing for the prohibition of sex work frequently justify the exclusion of these sex workers on the basis that sex workers and their allies are in league with the owners (often male) of the sex industry and acting to defend their interests.[14] The vast majority of sex workers in collectives such as SWOU and x:talk are either independent workers or work in conditions of employment under an employer in a brothel, agency or strip club. It is due to this lack of class analysis that critics of sex workers' self-organising are frequently unable to draw an analytical distinction between workers and owners of the industry. Workers who speak out are branded part of the 'pro-prostitution' or 'pro-sex work' lobby or as 'paid internet shills', despite the fact that there is an important political and class distinction between being in favour of an industry and wanting to change your conditions within it.[15] X:talk and Sex Workers Open University workers' collectives are populated solely by workers across a broad spectrum of the industry.

The alignment of interests of workers' with the 'industry' is also promulgated by official decisions relating to who is selected to speak on issues pertaining to sex work. Vida (26, white British), who had not been involved in any campaigning around the issue, read the transcripts from the House of Commons meeting, noting the fact that no dancers had been invited to share their case and that it was:

> only industry operators, Peter Stringfellow and his flunkies and there was girls up in the audience and at one point he says 'well we've got our girls if you want to speak to them, we'll arrange an interview'. Like that smacks of ownership and control and you know it makes him sound like a pimp. And that public debate in that arena, in that fucking Houses of Parliament, like why are lap dancers not being given a voice here?
>
> (Vida, 26, white British)

Vida, like most other dancers, distinguishes between dancers' (workers') voices and those of 'industry operators' of managers, employers and owners of clubs and contests the ability of them to speak in dancers' interests. This contests the frequent claim that dancers or other sex workers who assert that the way they earn money constitutes 'work' are mouthpieces of the sex industry. As one activist puts it: 'am I interested in defending the sex industry? Not at all. Am I interested in defending sex workers? Of course, and the distinction is important' (x:talk activist cited in Cruz 2013: 470).

The case of Hackney and the attempt to close down strip clubs elsewhere through the new licensing regime presents a sobering example of the (unforeseen?) effects of such legalistic tactics. In threatening the existence of their workplaces, dancers were forced to align their interests with those of club owners in order to defend their workplaces. Such alignment dampens the inherent antagonisms between workers and those who manage their work and extract surplus value from them, potentially undermining the possibility for wider transformation of their working conditions on more favourable terms to the dancers. Such conditions make it impossible for dancers to discuss or challenge the exploitation without it being used against them. Feminist Fightback state that they 'supports the right of sex workers to organise amongst themselves to *fight exploitation* in the sex industry and transform the conditions under which they work' (our emphasis).[16] Self-organisation of workers and contestation of the terms of exploitation are rarely in the interests of bosses and industry owners. In dismissing dancers' and other sex workers' self-organisation as industry representation, workers are denied the ability to organise *against* their bosses.

Similarly dangerously, discourses which argue for the wholesale closure of the industry homogenise workplaces within an industry characterised by highly variable conditions, housing both good management and highly exploitative conditions. Such homogenisation disguises rather than highlights the practices of exploitation. As Emma (31, Belgian) opined: 'there are some places where people are exploited. I'm sure there are horror stories to be told, but it's very dangerous to tar all the places with the same brush.' Further, Suzanna (38, white British) argued that 'Hackney tradition' in particular was a better model for ensuring women's relative autonomy in their workplace: 'Browns and the White Horse let the dancers sort themselves out ... this is the exception and this is where the possibility for change is glimpsed. So [maintaining] the particularity of the Hackney traditions is really crucial.' As such, the campaign in Hackney focused on the closure of clubs with better conditions for dancers than the high levels of control and surveillance of more corporate chains, who faced no such threat to their existence.

The sex workers' rights organisations who seek to organise workers from within the industry begin from a position which understands sex work – including stripping – as a complex phenomenon produced through multiple structuring factors including women's place in the labour market, labour migration controls and gendered and sexual relations. For them, the key class alliance is that between the working class. These activists locate transformation of the sex industry and people's experiences in it through struggle in the workplace on the one hand and much wider social and economic change on the other. They call (first) for a 'living wage, recognising unpaid labour of women, or all reproductive labour' (x:talk activist cited in Cruz 2013: 471), as well as 'a world without borders and papers for all migrants' (GMB activist) in addition to decriminalisation and legal approaches which can improve working conditions for women (and men and transpeople) in the sex industry.

For these organisations and activists, exploitation (in the traditional Marxist sense) remains as important as representation in struggles for gender (and class) equality, while in the 'new feminism' of Object 'cultural domination supplants exploitation as the fundamental injustice' (Fraser 1995: 68). While Object represents strip clubs as an issue of gender equality, the answer to which is their abolition, this does not recognise the competing theories of gender equality, such as those posed by dancers and other sex workers themselves. The subordination of women in this sense is understood purely as a result of sexual imagery, rather in addition to the relationship between paid and unpaid work and capitalism's wider division of labour which undervalues women's labour in the employment market (for example).

The feminism presented by Object is one totally denuded of any semblance of concern for class or the multiple other intersecting social categories which shape and constrain women's choices. It is striking that in Object's cultural rendering of the strip club question, the connections between the social and economic are entirely absent, as they choose instead to focus solely on the arena of culture and representation (see also McDowell 2001). Further, the class politics of Object have aligned with middle-class politics (perhaps inadvertently) with the interests of capital (both disembodied and embodied in the desires of the council) in revalorising working-class neighbourhoods As such, this makes a powerful 'urban ruling-class alliance' between the interests of capital in its disembodied form as well as embodied in the state and middle-class values about appropriate purposes for urban land use. Hackney is not an exception, as the pattern is exemplified in the initial case of Durham and more recently in Tower Hamlets (Chapter 3). Capital's interests are both disembodied in seeking out new urban land to generate exchange value and embodied in the interests of the new urban middle classes, as well as having interests represented in the borough council.

While Object represent themselves as a 'human rights' group, this universalisation of 'rights' disguises other power dynamics in which people are not similarly or equally situated in making claims, to the city or to sexual or bodily autonomy. Women are asymmetrically valued in these accounts. Object's style of feminist activism has focused on a choice number of spaces of women's rights and gender equality: the glass ceiling, violence against women and the sex industry (largely framed in the context of the latter). This has rendered some women's work (such as that of the professional classes) as 'real work' and worthy of activism in which to secure equality and fairness in the workplace, while constituting other women's work (such as that in the sex industry) as undesirable. Contrary to this, many voices in the sex workers' rights movement and amongst their allies in the feminist movement have been vocal about the ways in which the industry can be improved. These voices have located the production of the sex industry in much wider debates about the structural conditions and constraints in which women make agentic decisions, alongside a sexual libertarianism which asserts women's own bodily autonomy and sexual expression.

Conclusion

Strip clubs are simultaneously both sites of sexual expression and oppression and of possibilities for emancipation. These emancipatory strategies do not usually take the form of stripping *qua* stripping (with exceptions, such as for 'professionals' who find valuable sexual expression in the activity), but stripping as a strategic route out of the worse ends of the labour market or as part of strategies for upward mobility otherwise unavailable to them (Chapter 4). As such, the claim made by 'anti-lap dancing' campaigners such as those in Object that the new form of licensing will 'better protect' dancers has not only proven to be a fallacy but was never the intention of campaigns around strip clubs and in fact has the potential effect of foreclosing women's desires for personal autonomy, economic independence and bodily integrity.

The use of the law in any progressive political project 'inevitably implicated accommodation to our current forms of social and symbolic life' (Cornell 1995: 27) and limits the conditions for its wider transformation. In practice, the licensing has at best done nothing to improve the conditions of dancers and at worst has precluded dancers' attempts at self-determination, not least through the establishment of a co-operatively run venue. Using this legalistic approach has condemned women to remain in these asymmetrical and frequently exploitative relations. What's more, the feminist rhetoric is based on a universalist claim to gender equality aligned neatly with others to facilitate an ongoing process of urban revanchism.

Long-standing critiques of certain aspects of feminist organising and politics have sought to highlight the unequal and oppressive power relationships that can exist between women, as well as those based on gender difference. Black, working-class, gay and disabled feminists have pointed out the ways in which power relationships grounded in race, class and ability also intersect to influence the lives of women. These critiques of bourgeois and white feminism have largely been ignored in the campaigns of Object and others who have attempted to stake out the hegemonic feminist position on stripping, conceptualising it as violence against women and ignoring its structural and socio-economic foundations, rendering it a matter of culture and representation. In doing so, it fails to account for other intersecting modes of power, such as race and class and is devoid of any structural analysis of the factors and social relations which are productive of the labour supply into the stripping industry. Far from 'people power', in asserting this power through legalistic bureaucratic means, namely through the state, they have operated on a register of power which inherently necessitates knowledge of and confidence with processes of state bureaucracy, potentially excluding working-class or migrant individuals without the necessary language confidence or skills with which to engage with it.

The change in legislation may have offered an opportune moment to improve conditions for dancers in clubs across the UK, some of which, as outlined in this book, have extremely bad labour practices and operate through highly exploitative relations with dancers. Campaign groups' and legislators' refusal to meet with, speak to or even step foot in dancers' workplaces precluded the possibility that dancers could voice the actual conditions they wanted to transform. Instead, the new licensing has concentrated power in the hands of employers and away from workers. Despite this, there is already a feminist politics of stripping on the ground which foregrounds listening to the lived experiences of dancers. Since 'feminism is ultimately about politically taking the chance to create new worlds' (Cornell 1995: 27), legal projects which enjoin the state to intervene *on behalf* of women inherently impedes the development of a terrain of possibility for the transformation of women's lives and for creating those new worlds, in solidarity with dancers and sex workers, beginning from the very place in which they stand.

Notes

1 Object: www.object.org.uk/about-the-campaign.
2 A representative from Object declined to be interviewed, instead answering questions by email and directing us to its website.
3 Camille Paglia is a social and cultural theorist, known for her radically libertarian stance on issues, not limited to, but particularly including, sexuality (as well as abortion, suicide, drugs).
4 www.xtalkproject.net/?page_id=2.
5 Hackney Council Sex Establishment Licensing policy 2011: www.hackney.gov.uk/Assets/Documents/sex-establishment-licensing-2011.pdf.
6 Video 'Hands Off': http://hackneycitizen.co.uk/2010/12/15/hands-off-women-speak-out-over-hackney-strip-clubs/.
7 Hackney Sex Establishment Licensing Policy: mginternet.hackney.gov.uk/mgConvert2PDF.aspx?ID=12483.
8 See www.object.org.uk/morenews/110-lap-dancing-press-release-on-hackney-proposal-to-set-nil-limits for further testimonies.
9 Let's talk about sex says Hackney Council, *The Hackney Citizen*, 4 October 2010. Online: http://hackneycitizen.co.uk/2010/10/04/let%E2%80%99s-talk-about-sex-says-hackney-council/.
10 Anonymous woman, Object website: www.object.org.uk/morenews/110-lap-dancing-press-release-on-hackney-proposal-to-set-nil-limits.
11 Object: www.object.org.uk/about-the-campaign.
12 See Feminist Fightback for more on this debate within the London feminist movement: www.feministfightback.org.uk/?cat=11.
13 www.storify.com/fornicatrix/left-out-in-the-cold-sex-workers-at-notts-womens-s.
14 See, for example, Cath Elliott on the International Union of Sex Workers, www.toomuchtosayformyself.com/2009/01/09/the-great-iusw-con/; the reply from Feminist Fightback, www.feministfightback.org.uk/?p=102; and also, www.ruthjacobs.co.uk/2013/01/25/nicole-rowe-feminist-activists-co-founder-nordic-model-advocates-normas/.
15 www.ruthjacobs.co.uk/2013/01/25/nicole-rowe-feminist-activists-co-founder-nordic-model-advocates-normas/.
16 www.feministfightback.org.uk/?p=102.

References

Adkins, L. (1995) *Gender Work, Sexuality, Family and Labour Market*, Milton Keynes and Philadelphia: Open University Press.
Barton, B. (2000) *Stripped: Inside the Lives of Erotic Dancers*, New York: New York University Press.

Butler, T. (2002) Thinking global but acting local: the middle classes in the city, *Sociological Research Online* 7 (3). Online: www.socresonline.org.uk/7/3/timbutler.html.

Cacciottolo, M. (2012) London 2012: will the Olympics bring more prostitutes?, *BBC News Magazine*, 7 June. Online: www.bbc.co.uk/news/magazine-18174387.

Chun, S. (1999) An uncommon alliance: finding empowerment for exotic dancers through labor unions, *Hastings Women's Law Journal* 10 (1): 231–52.

Cornell, D. (1995) *The Imaginary Domain: Abortion, Pornography and Sexual Harassment*, New York: Routledge.

Cruz, K. (2013) Unmanageable work, (un)liveable lives: the UK sex industry, labour rights and the welfare state, *Social & Legal Studies* 22 (4): 465–88.

Dean, J. (2012) On the march or on the margins? Affirmations and erasures of feminist activism in the UK, *European Journal of Women's Studies* 19 (3): 315–29.

Dworkin, A. (1989) *Pornography: Men Possessing Women*, London: Penguin.

Fraser, N. (1995) From redistribution to recognition? Dilemmas of justice in a 'post-socialist' age, *New Left Review*, I/212, July–August. Online: http://newleftreview.org/I/212/nancy-fraser-from-redistribution-to-recognition-dilemmas-of-justice-in-a-post-socialist-age.

Gillespie, T. (2013) *Accumulation by Urban Dispossession: Struggles over Urban Space in Accra, Ghana*, unpublished PhD thesis, University of Leeds.

Glass, R. (1964) *Introduction to London: Aspects of Change*, London:: Centre for Urban Studies (reprinted in Glass, R. (1989) *Clichés of Urban Doom*, Oxford: Blackwell, pp. 132–158).

Harvey, D. (1989) *The Urban Experience*, Baltimore, MD: Johns Hopkins University Press.

Hubbard, P. and Colosi, R. (2013) Sex, crime and the city: municipal law and the regulation of sexual entertainment, *Social and Legal Studies* 22 (1): 67–86.

Lees, L. (2000) A reappraisal of gentrification: towards a 'geography of gentrification', *Progress in Human Geography* 24 (3): 389–408.

Hayashi-Danns, J. and Leveque, S. (2011) *Stripped: The Bare Reality of Lap Dancing*, East Sussex: Clairview Books.

Hughes, K. and Tadic, V. (1998) Something to deal with: customer sexual harassment and women's retail service work in Canada, *Gender, Work and Organization* 5 (4): 207–19.

Jessop, B. (2002) Liberalism, neo-liberalism and urban governance: a state theoretical perspective, *Antipode* 34 (3): 452–72.

Mackinnon, C. (1989) Sexuality, pornography, and method: 'pleasure under patriarchy', *Ethics* 314: 99.

McDowell, L. (2001) Father and Ford revisited: gender, class and employment change in the new millennium, *Transactions of the Institute of British Geographers* 26 (4): 448–64.

Mitchell, D. (2003) *The Right to the City: Social Justice and the Fight for Public Space*, New York: The Guildford Press.

Osborne, L. (2011) Vicar hits out at council's ban on lapdancing clubs, *The Independent*, 30 January. Online: www.independent.co.uk/news/uk/politics/vicar-hits-out-at-councils-ban-on-lapdancing-clubs-2198449.html.

Peachey, P. (2012) How the Olympic clean-up put sex workers in danger: an increase in police raids over the past 18 months has seen prostitutes moved on, *The Independent*, 12 May. Online: www.independent.co.uk/sport/olympics/how-the-olympic-cleanup-put-sex-workers-in-danger-7737986.html.

Sassen, S. (1991) *The Global City*, Princeton: Princeton University Press.

Segal, L. and McIntosh, M. (eds) (1992) Sex Exposed: *Sexuality and the Pornography Debate*, London: Virago.

Seymour, B. (2009) Shoreditch and the creative destruction of the inner city, *Variant*, 34. Online: www.variant.org.uk/pdfs/issue34/shoreditch34.pdf.

Shrage, L. (1994) *Moral Dilemmas of Feminism: Prostitution, Adultery, and Abortion*, Abingdon: Routledge.

Shrage, L. (2005) Exposing the fallacies of anti-porn feminism, *Feminist Theory* 6 (1): 45–65.

Smith, N. (1996) *The New Urban Frontier: Gentrification and the Revanchist City*, London: Routledge.

Thorpe, V. (2013) What now for Britain's new-wave feminists – after page 3 and £10 notes?, *The Guardian*, 27 July. Online: www.theguardian.com/world/2013/jul/27/new-generation-of-feminists-set-agenda.

Williams, C. (2003) Sky service: the demands of emotional labour in the airline industry, *Gender, Work and Organization* 10 (5): 513–50.

Conclusions: proliferation, stagnation or decline?

The UK strip industry now and beyond

The stripping industry is both heterogeneous and dynamic and is responsive to fluctuations in the broader social, economic and political conditions and relations by which it is constituted. In moving between different scales of the production and regulation of the stripping industry, in this book we have looked beyond micro-sociologies of stripping work. Instead we offer a multi-scalar, holistic approach, moving from examining the individual orientations to examining the labour processes inside clubs; the discursive landscape in which current legislation was shaped; the broader politics that surround stripping and its constitution through constellations of law (legislation), economics (political economy) and social relations, including contemporary gender relations.

Our contribution firmly places dancers and their working conditions at the centre of our investigation, moving across micro-, meso- and macro-levels of analysis. At the micro-scale we examined dancers' subjective experiences and the materiality of working in strip venues, as well as the particular form of labour that is performed and consumed there. At the meso-level, the structure and operations of the clubs have been interrogated, to investigate the roles of managers and internal logics of accumulation and value extraction inside the clubs. In turn, we examined how these micro- and meso-levels interact with the macro-scale processes, including the regulatory licensing framework and the contemporary labour market, to produce the current landscape of striptease as a site of labour and consumption in the UK economy.

Drawing together the different elements from the research, we make five key arguments. First, we address the claim that the industry was exponentially proliferating prior to the introduction of the new legislation and that this was due to a growth in demand. We argue instead that the growth of the industry is attributable to a labour supply of women seeking relatively high-paid, flexible work, the privatisation of higher education and the marketisation of other credentials, the changing nature of consumption in urban centres and the night-time economy, and the cultural mimesis of 'City' culture. Importantly, our central thesis is that a key reason for the expansion of the industry is the way in which clubs have been able to profit from dancers' desire or need to work in the industry through exponential fee increases and limitless numbers of women put on the rota to work on any given night.

Second, we problematise the claim that stripping work has been 'mainstreamed', by emphasising the continuing (and renewed) stigma that dancers face and argue that an affective experience of mainstreaming (i.e. the *sense* that strip clubs are proliferating) may be as much to do with exposure to venues due to new classed spatial patterns of urban centres as with actual quantitative expansion. That is, we believe the claim of exponential increase in strip club – called the 'growing tide' – may be as much to do with the visibility of adult entertainment in town centres and gentrifying neighbourhoods: quantitative expansion. In relation to discussions about the current state of the industry, we make some speculative claims about the future of the industry, arguing that it may already have reached its zenith, as it loses its novelty and as SEV licensing limits the opening of new venues and the renewal of some existing licences. We also argue, however, that without fundamental transformation of the conditions in which women live, namely the compulsion to undertake wage labour and a lack of viable options for well-paid, flexible labour, the industry will find a continuous supply of workers to work in it and to support its permanence through their payment of fees.

Third, we argue that in terms of regulation, although the new world of SEV licensing borne out of the anti-lap dancing campaigns to close down the industry has made little change to date, it may by default have enabled a new form of licensing which has the potential to in fact improve working conditions. There is evidence that the powers under the SEV licensing regime can use licensing in order to put in place conditions for the benefit of dancers' well-being.

Fourth, dancers' voices have, to date, been buried within both mainstream feminist politics around dancing and in legislative processes. The research presented here places dancers' voices centre stage and draws on them to develop a better understanding of the ways in which dancers' understand their labour, their reasons for working in the industry and the context in which they work. Put simply, most dancers see their work as neither degrading nor empowering, but instead engage in it as wage labour, which is experienced in varying ways. Fifth, we argue that 'feminist' activist approaches to stripping are characterised by their desire for the erasure of strip clubs and stripping work from society – this approach is not hegemonic. Other feminist projects are underway which are grounded in solidarity between dancers and other feminists and are characterised by intersectional analyses of stripping work and an approach which seeks to understand both structural factors and dancers' agency in their engagement in stripping work and the social relations in which it takes place.

What produced the expansion of the stripping industry?

The stripping industry has grown out a series of interlocking social, economic and cultural factors which have culminated in producing a climate in which adult entertainment has moved out of the backstreets – or from behind the smoke screens of the exclusive high-end hostess club – and into the high streets for the (usually male) masses. Such 'massification' (in terms of both labour and consumption) has been facilitated by cultures of conspicuous consumption, the inherent tendency in capitalism for relentless commodification and the liberalisation of licensing laws, as well as a formal labour market hostile to young women. The 'nocturnalisation' of accumulation and consumption provided the material and discursive landscape for strip clubs to arise, alongside the growth of other spaces of night-time leisure (Koslofsky 2011; see also Chapter 2 this volume). The integration of services and leisure industries as an integral part of the contemporary UK economy has expanded the prevalence of employment patterns characterised by temporary, casual and twenty-four hour work patterns (Hobbs et al. 2000). As such, the expansion of erotic dance venues in town centres must be understood in terms of a broader expansion of service industries and a diversified night-time economy as a key site of 'growth' and profit (Brents and Sanders 2010).

Such accumulation in night-time spaces has been accompanied by a more generalised expansion of a gendered labour market characterised by multiple forms of intimate and care services, including sexualised services (see collection by Wolkowitz et al. 2013). Indeed, it is the nature of the wider labour market in the UK which has shaped labour supply into stripping. While a minority of dancers ('professionals') were attracted to dancing specifically for its occupational identity and its freedom of expression and artistry, the majority of dancers engaged in dancing more strategically. Many used dancing to fund greater attainment and the credentials necessary for mobility in a highly competitive labour market, others for capital accumulation for other aspirational projects (usually to fund the establishment of small businesses). It should be emphasised that, for most dancers, the nature of stripping as a relatively highly paid *and* flexible form of work was the key attraction.

Dramatic inequalities of wealth in the UK and between the UK and countries such as Romania and Brazil (the two core sender countries in our study) constitute stripping work as a space in which dancers can engage in order to facilitate future-orientated aspirations which may otherwise be out of reach. The low level of entry into the industry, due to the opening up of the labour market and its 'deskilling', make stripping an accessible labour market and one which can be considered less 'risky' than other areas of sex industry, due to greater levels of regulatory control and surveillance. Broader labour market conditions are unfavourable for young women. It is estimated that 850,000 jobs will be cut from the public sector between 2010 and 2017, with 'obvious implications for the sector's relatively feminised workforce' (Felstead et al. 2012). These jobs, which have traditionally provided higher quality employment for women in terms and condition and job security, are not likely to return, even in the context of economic upturn. In addition, a House of Commons gender audit found that 80 per cent of budgetary cuts and new tax revenue from austerity measures would come directly from women. Since austerity appears to have become a hegemonic principle amongst the major political parties, it is unlikely that these effects on women will be reversed in the near future. Finally, as work intensity increases in the UK, especially for women (Felstead et al. 2012), formal, mainstream employment options may appear less favourable than the informal economy, including the stripping industry or other sex industries, which may be able to offer higher rates of pay, more flexible work through which to pursue other aspirations and more autonomy within the work-place (in some cases) (Sanders 2013).

In addition to such macro-economic factors, the ways in which dancers' labour is organised and value is extracted in strip clubs has laid the basis for further expansion of the industry, often with minimal risk for those investing in it. Clubs have no obligation to provide work for dancers or to provide any base level of income, giving managers ultimate numerical flexibility – the ability to rota as many dancers as they choose per shift. High fee rates and unlimited flexibility incentivises managers to maximise the number of dancers working on each shift. These high numbers of dancers intensify competition between women and reduce wages, a process which was compounded in the context of declining demand (see below). John Gray, owner of super-chain Spearmint Rhino, explicitly admitted that the impact of recession and the reduction in demand in strip clubs affected the dancers, while not affecting club owners: 'in the U.K., this [recession] largely affects the dancers' income and not the clubs as the dancers are independent' (Ellyatt 2013: no page). As such, many strip clubs themselves have managed to remain buoyant in recession, while dancers themselves feel the effects of over-supply of labour, high fee rates and reductions in demand. Such economics have enabled clubs to open and remain resilient regardless of the level of demand or custom they acquire.

The UK strip industry is constituted by individual clubs with internal markets in which risk is shifted to workers, while club owners benefit directly from danc-ers' house fees, as well as from various other sources of value production – both from the dancers themselves and from the customers. So, through fees, fines and commission from dancers, the club makes revenue and profit regardless of the sale of customer entrance fees and over-priced drinks. Workers' adopt the finan-cial risk, as there is no guarantee of income and many women often leave a shift just breaking even on their overheads or even in debt (see Chapter 4). Therefore, as we have suggested elsewhere 'far from proliferating as a response to demand, the [stripping] industry has maintained its market presence due to its ability to establish highly financially exploitative employment relationships with dancers at a time of economic fragility' (Sanders and Hardy 2012: 513). It should be noted that such patterns are not unique to the stripping industry, but can also be noted in the employment relations of taxi drivers and personal trainers, amongst others, although the disjuncture between fees and possibilities for earning appear to be particularly acute in the stripping industry.

As such, a key argument we have made is that this economic structure of value extraction in the stripping industry is a key reason for the proliferation in terms of quantitative numbers of venues. These structures, however, have also had a signif-icant impact on the changing nature of the labour itself and therefore of women's experiences in it. We have conceptualised this as 'the race to the bottom'. The shift from traditional striptease to private dancing with the introduction of 'gentlemen's clubs' in the 1990s transformed processes of value extraction, as clubs shifted to requiring fees from dancers in order to perform. From the advent of the recession in 2008, rather than increase door entry prices or the cost of dances, with the potential effect of losing custom, clubs began to 1) raise the price of fees and 2) raise the number of women working at any one time (and paying fees). This had the result of heightening competition between dancers and, we argue, ultimately reducing the standards, conditions and wages as a result. In order to secure valuable custom and to make enough to cover the costs of fees and other associated costs, it is argued by many dancers that other dancers intensified their work by offering more than the regulated dance. By performing 'extras', dancers were forced to undercut each other in this 'race to the bottom' in order to sustain their income.

Moving beyond simplistic accounts of 'objectification' as explanations for the desire to consume stripping labour, we have argued that at the root of this consumption is a desire for relationality, attention and recognition, as well as some forms of objectification (not least due to the objectifying nature of the wage relation). This colours both customers' desire to be recognised by the dancer and customers' desires to be recognised by others in homo-social relations through their engagement with women. In doing so, we point to the relational work that is undertaken by dancers in negotiating the particular form of attention that is to be commodified and the type of affective labour (sexualised, emotional or deferential) that delivers it. In locating this in the growing contemporary attention economies, we align it with other emergent systems of value production in contemporary capitalism.

Rather than a simple growth in misogynistic desire for female objectification through sexual entertainment or a general mainstreaming of a sexualised culture (Levy 2005) – the argument foregrounded by many anti-lap dancing campaigners (Jeffreys 2008: 151) – we argue that it is these interlocking legal, cultural and macro-economic processes which have led to the expansion of the stripping industry. Whilst there is clearly a demand and market for stripping as 'adult entertainment', the reasons for the growth and permanence of the industry are manifold (see also Sanders and Hardy 2012) and can only be fully understood and therefore addressed in their full complexity.

Troubling the 'mainstreaming' thesis

Object and others grounded their campaign to ban 'lap dancing' on the notion that the stripping industry was being 'mainstreamed' and 'normalised'.[1] While Brents and Sanders (2010) and others have demonstrated empirical examples of such processes, the precise meaning of the concept of 'mainstreaming' remains unclear. Its use appears to have been consistently and cumulatively conceptually stretched in order to incorporate the representation of stripping in popular culture, the spatial relocation of venues to city centres (seemingly conjured as the site of 'mainstream' consumption), the quantitative increase in consumption of stripping, and growing legitimacy and acceptability of women's labour in the stripping industry.

While there has been a quantitative increase in the number of strip club *venues*, there are two important points to note about this apparent 'expansion'. First, it is likely there has also been *felt* intensification due to the changing spatialities of both strip club venues and also middle-class lifestyles. It is not only the numeral increase in venues but also their shifting presence into spaces of middle-class consumption that has caused anxiety. For example, due to the gentrification of town centres and of working-class neighbourhoods, such as the Borough of Hackney, London (see Chapter 8), stripping is increasingly located in spaces which are frequented by the middle classes. Second, the number of venues does not reflect actual levels of consumption. Increased venues does not mean that more customers are necessarily engaging in the consumption of striptease or that small numbers of customers are engaging in *more* frequent or quantitative consumption. In fact, during the three years in which we spent time in venues, they were frequently empty, or extremely quiet, particularly during the week and dancers themselves reported declining 'demand'. It would not be unreasonable therefore to postulate that demand may well have peaked during the boom years that ended with the economic crash of 2008.

With regard to claims that stripping is increasingly seen as a legitimate, acceptable and 'normalised' job, dancers in fact claimed that stigma had increased in recent years. This was attributed to the labelling of strip clubs as part of the 'sex industries' and also due to campaigns which have sought to represent dancing as a harmful practice for women, in which women are victimised and lack autonomy. Dalia (20, white British) said that she would leave the industry if it became labelled as part of the sex industries, adding that: 'the girls don't want to dance if that [sex workers] is what they're going to be labelled as, it's already enough of a taboo'. Edie (33, white British), who had worked for over a decade as a stripper, said that she had seen the stigma around dancing shift and return again: 'you used to say you were a pole dancer and people would high five you and now they say "really? Oh my god"'.

As Dalia and Edie describe, the effects of anti-stripping campaigns have been to increase the stigma faced by the women who work in the industry. This contests the 'mainstreaming' thesis, which claims that dancing is increasingly acceptable and legitimate and in fact shows evidence to the contrary. Such stigma furthers the silencing of dancers and – perhaps more dangerously – dissuades them from speaking out about exploitation or abuse that they may face in the workplace. Laura (28, white British), an ex-dancer now working as a solicitor, said that she had once told some colleagues that she used to dance, but that she regretted it and now would not tell anyone else. Living with such secrecy, in a 'double life' reflects the experiences of many sex workers (Sanders 2005). The consequences of stigma manifest themselves in the lack of power that dancers (and other sex workers) have to disclose harassment, unfair working practices and recourse to official intervention from the police, for instance. The legislation introduced under the Policing and Crime Act was designed to contest and reverse the mainstreaming of the stripping industry, yet while it has failed to dislodge its economic significance in the night-time economy, it has served to increase stigma that dancers face.

Despite this, there is evidence that the sex industry is being mainstreamed in everyday life for increasing numbers of people, although this is through economics rather than legal or cultural processes. Indeed, Swerling (2013) reports that there are more women entering prostitution as a result of austerity measures. If we

consider the raising of university fees to £9,000 a year as one of the earlier austerity measures and the retrenchment of the state as proto-austerity, even before
the crisis of 2008, all these processes sustain and stimulate the labour supply into
the stripping industry. Legalistic means are therefore not sufficient in challenging
the 'mainstreaming' of the stripping and wider sex industries. If achieving gender
equality is the main objective in the politics of stripping, a more holistic understanding is required of the ways in which dancing and other informal work, particularly in the sex industry, is mainstreamed into women's strategies for survival,
ambition and economic independence. The goal of greater autonomy, freedom
and equality for women cannot be achieved simply through contesting 'normal-
ising discourses', but through attending to the material and structural processes
which shape the context in which women make decisions about their lives.

The future of stripping?

The industry is by no means static, shaped as it is by the changing economic environment in which it is constituted, as well as changing legal frameworks, political
contexts, gender relations and trends in leisure and consumption. It should be
noted that this study took place during a particular time frame (2010–13) during
which the recession had taken hold and the industry was responding to campaigns
to close it down, eventually culminating in the new legislation. Dancers, managers
and owners in the research all stated that the recession had taken its toll and the
industry had shrunk in terms of custom and revenue (although not necessarily the
number of clubs, see above). Several dancers spoke about the impact of the recession. Heidi (26, white British) said that for individuals 'I think it's not a necessity
any more, it's more of a luxury. If you're going to cut back on anything it's going
to be going to the lap dancing clubs.' Nina (26, white British) also referred to belt-
tightening in the corporate sector, a previously important source of income:

> There used to be loads of [corporate money], hence being able to make loads
> of money on a weekday years ago, but since the recession, they've cut back
> luxuries … It stopped because people aren't bringing in … people haven't got
> the money to do that anymore, to schmooze them.

The expansion of the stripping industry ran in parallel to – and a result of – the
boom years from the late 1990s to 2007/2008. It is clear that the advent of the
'deepest and most protracted global economic crisis after 1929' (Karamessini
2014) in 2008 has abruptly put the brakes on the expansion of the industry across
the UK, leading to decreasing demand within it. This effect is not evenly spread,
however, either geographically or across the sector itself. While elite consumption has once again risen, with demand for luxury goods increasing year on year
(Ellyatt 2013; Neate 2013), the average worker has seen a significant reduction
in real wages and therefore in disposable income. Yet City bonuses remain buoyant and the super rich remain unaffected or have in fact gained from the growing
disparities of wealth (Hughes 2013). The top 1 per cent of earners have seen their

wealth increase from 7 per cent in the mid-1990s to 10 per cent in 2013, rising steadily even through – or especially because of – recession (Stewart 2013). Growing wages at the top of the labour market, stagnant wages at the bottom and dramatic falls in real wages creates ripe conditions for generating an almost inexhaustible labour supply into the stripping industry. With wealth concentrated in the capital of London and with regions (particularly in the north of England) harder hit by cuts and retrenchment, it can be expected that the higher end of the stripping industry based in London will remain resilient. Strip clubs in the heart of the capital report continued consumption, albeit with a shift in its constellation. As corporate entertainment accounts are curtailed and jobs are lost in the lower echelons of the financial sector, even with steady attendance, customers are consuming fewer dances than before. It is likely that this will lead to an uneven geography of spending between central London clubs catering to wealthy diasporas and financial workers and a decline in demand amongst middle-income and low-income earners, particularly in regional areas.

In addition to the changing economic context, the new era of SEV licensing is likely to lead to club closures, as local authority licensing committees use their new powers to act out either their own ideological interests or urban 'regeneration' projects, or are harangued by pressure groups to impose restrictions on the location of strip clubs. Yet the extent to which this will curb the numbers of strip clubs is yet to be seen. At the time of writing (September 2013) there were over 250 clubs licensed under the new SEV licensing process, and this does not account for the unlicensed activities that take place. On the whole, therefore, the number of clubs may remain fairly similar to that of the boom period in the 1990s.

Licensing as SEVs may reduce the number of clubs in the UK, but it will not stop the accumulation of large amounts of capital by the clubs that remain, which may even been fortified in their control over women who have fewer choices about where to sell their labour. We have clearly shown there are possibilities for change under the SEV licensing regime, as licensing committees have the option to take account of dancers' needs into consideration. As detailed in Chapter 7, there are several examples of good practice whereby SEV policies have considered the health, safety and well-being of the dancer. Such conditions include: banning of fines; improving safety by banning closed-off booths; improving security for dancers; and ensuring appropriate facilities are provided for dancers. The conditions imposed by the licensing of clubs (and their enactment in practice) make a fundamental difference to safety and well-being inside clubs, as does their physical layout and many dancers further emphasised the importance of female managers. Through our impact project, in which we mobilised the research to influence evidence-based policy, we have demonstrated that there is the potential for the improvement of working conditions. Importantly, for dancers organising in their workplaces, we have shown through direct work with licensing committees that it is at this meso-level in which there is leverage in order to demand change in the industry to even out balances of power between club management and dancers and reduce practices of exploitation (see Chapter 7).

As such, the combination of stricter licensing, less demand in the economy at large, alongside sustained demand in the luxury markets of central London may lead to a changing geography of strip club work and consumption in the UK. Despite these changes, strip clubs still seem remarkably resilient, even in the context of resistance from ideological objectors, increased scrutiny and legislation and ongoing economic crisis. We argue this is in part due to the labour supply of women, who, in an absence of alternative relatively well-paid, highly flexible jobs will continue to pay fees in order to work in clubs in hope of that one high-paying customer.

Regulation: dancers as body parts, not as workers

The story of the rise (and fall?) of lap dancing is as much the story of the rise of finance capital and city culture and its conspicuous consumption as of the changing political-economic forms which iteratively transform the use of urban space. Concerns about the actors and practices associated with night-time city spaces have historical precedents, as the city by night is seen to clash with its daytime civic purpose (Walkowitz 1992). Despite its renaissance as an important time-space of accumulation and even as neo-liberalism encourages its subjects to live as puritans by day and hedonists by night (Bell [1976] 1996), the night remains associated with transgression and urban space is seen to rightfully belong to the 'productive' day (Koslofsky 2011). As secondary waves of gentrification roll in over towns and cities in the UK, the venues and spaces of night-time culture that played an important role in the initial valorisation of urban space are successively removed through complaints and revoking of licences.

Hubbard et al. (2009:186) note how the regulation of sex and sexually orientated businesses is increasingly taking place through licensing laws, as: 'licensing constitutes a site of struggle in which different constituencies fight to have their understanding of what is appropriate land-use legitimated'. The local powers in the SEV policies are being utilised to limit the number of clubs – or in a minority of cases close them down by not renewing licences – on the basis that they are 'out of place'. Much of this contestation reflects that of other urban struggles over land use, involving local residents and fears of lawlessness and loss of social control, related to night-time governance and alcohol consumption more generally. The gendered and sexualised nature of the activities within the venues, however, add another layer to the political debates around the 'place' of strip venues in contemporary urban landscapes. Yet the focus on gender and objectification disguise the class politics of the attempts to erase these venues from the night-time economy. Object's campaign has neatly intertwined with class interests, including state-led gentrification and the construction of urban centres which appeal to middle-class tastes and orientations.

Yet whilst there is a clear argument that the venue is 'out of place' and hence the venue is presented as the target for new legislation, we question whether this is the complete story in the regulation of stripping and indeed all commercial sex activities.

Jackson (2011) shows how the dancer is sexualised in general licensing protocol and conditions, that her labour is not considered but instead she is considered only by her body parts (breasts, genitalia, anus and so on), resulting in her body *qua* worker ignored. As Jackson's (2011) analysis of stripping legislation in Las Vegas similarly concludes, our analysis shows that whilst the public discourses are about the 'out of place' *venues* ('lap dancing' NIMBYism), evidence suggests the consternation over stripping is actually underpinned by which *bodies* are considered inappropriate and 'out of place' in the 'community' (Chapters 3, 7 and 8). It is the female body (of the stripper) that is heavily restricted and regulated through the licensing laws, as these bodies are considered out of place, in need of controlling and corruptive of ordinary civil behaviours. The law deals very directly with restrictions on nudity and controlling other aspects of sexual, sensual and erotic behaviour as we testify in Chapter 7.

Those who call for 'nil policies' conjure up images of an imagined community, the borders of which explicitly excludes dancers. Calls for strip clubs to be closed down and attempts to eliminate the industry essentially render sex workers as external to the 'community', in contrast to the mother figure, for whom the urban landscape must be remade. In the case of licensing striptease, the club as workplace slips through the cracks and dancers are 'othered' from the very community in which they work (and often live). The notion of 'community' automatically excludes women who work as dancers, reproducing the age-old Madonna/Whore binary in which women are divided, judged, stigmatised and valued on the basis of their sexuality and sexual behaviour. In this case, such exclusion is actualised through legalistic means which privilege the particular subject position of the non-sex working woman, while denigrating the subject position and practices of the Other.

Dancers' voices: regulation, labour and experiences

Despite the lengthy public debates, parliamentary and ministerial time dedicated to introducing SEV licensing under the Policing and Crime Act 2009, dancers voices have tended to be missing, ignored or silenced. We outline how and why this has happened in Chapter 3, but it is poignant in these concluding thoughts to highlight the effect of these missing voices and to highlight the core messages they offer when they speak *and* we listen. The absence of dancers was notable during the reform. Throughout select committee hearings, no voice was given to those who currently worked in the industry, instead accepting the owners of major chains to speak on behalf of the 'industry'. Workers do not have the same interests as industry owners and are more easily discredited than dancers speaking about their own lived experiences. With no dancers to talk about their (varied) experiences of working in the stripping industry, and to highlight the areas where legislation and regulation could improve working conditions, these issues have never featured in the reforms. As regulatory assessments, criteria and the licensing process do not examine the strip clubs as workplaces, dancers have been left open to financial exploitation, arbitrary disciplinary measures and few employment rights.

Katy concisely summed up the attitude of the majority of women working in the stripping industry when she said: 'people say it's degrading, but I wouldn't go as far as to say it's empowering. But it's not degrading either' (Katy, 25, white British). This contests representations of the debate around stripping which consistently elide the argument that stripping constitutes a form of work with the argument that it is 'empowering'. The question of whether waged work generally is 'empowering' in any circumstances is a highly contested one, it is not clear why stripping would be any different. All of the women in the study opted for stripping work in a specific context in a wage economy, in which opting out of wage labour is an option only for the very few and in which all must sell their labour in order to reproduce themselves. The varying social categories which shaped women's compulsion to sell their labour, such as individuals' class status and educational attainment, interpolated them differently into the labour market, offering them varying degrees of power to choose alternatives.

Feminist politics of stripping

As Chapter 8 has shown, there is not only one 'feminist' approach to stripping. The activism and the feminist voices of strippers and their allies show an alternative approach to the dominant narrative of abolition. The fact that the introduction of SEV policies and the subsequent 'nil' policies in places such as Hackney may have now precluded the possibilities for dancers to organise their work independently vindicates the argument that despite overtures to interest in improving conditions for dancers, this campaign and ideological approach more generally promotes a particular type of gender equality, for a particular type of woman. This cultural feminism which privileges imagery and representation as key sites of oppression disregards the material conditions which produce dancing in particular and sex work in general as a lucrative labour market option for women. The context in which women – and all workers – must sell their labour is becoming more hostile through austerity measures in the UK. Women are particularly vulnerable to austerity due to their over reliance on the public sector as a site of high-quality work, which has experienced pay freeze and job losses (Karamessini 2014). Austerity and the retrenchment of the state has an infamously detrimental effect on gender equality, reducing the possibilities for women's employment while increasing the unpaid social reproduction they have to perform as the state shrinks. It is not clear how the restriction or removal of a site of lucrative and flexible employment for women operates as a vehicle for the achievement of gender equality in such conditions.

Object's campaigns construct 'woman' as 'a singly determined gendered subject' (Brown 2000: 208), in which other structures of oppression (race, class, sexuality) are disappeared from view. This presents an anaemic feminism, unable to account for other intersecting relations of power and domination, which may be experienced as more oppressive by non-white, non-middle-class, non-straight women and feminists. This is part of a much broader history of theoretical debates within feminism which has been 'torn apart by deeply contested ideas about how the values of liberty and equality are best expressed in terms of feminist aspirations ... in "sex" and "erotic life"' (Cornell 1995: 24). Some dancers did speak of the emancipatory nature of their sexual expression in the strip club. More, however, expressed its emancipatory potential in the economic independence it offered from parents or lovers or freedom from low-paid service work. All these representations contest the unitary vision of emancipation that Object speaks of in dancers' name.

A key category that has been missing from these mainstream feminist analyses of the stripping industry is that of class. As Chapter 4 indicates, for many dancers, the strip club represents a site in which class aspirations play out, albeit mediated by the class position from which the dancer enters the strip club. For working-class women, without high levels of education, stripping represented an opportunity to avoid the destiny of low-wage, unskilled service sector jobs, which constitute a growing sector of the economy and particularly of jobs that are being created in the post-recession years of continuing crisis and austerity. For women with more social and cultural capital, the strip club represented a site from which to enable their aspirations for class mobility or sustaining their location in the class hierarchy through paying for education with the hope of propelling them into the top half of the hourglass labour market. In a context in which inequalities are growing *between* women, as well as between men and women (McDowell 2012), making gender the 'single axis' by which stripping work is understood and therefore organised around, both fails to provide an analysis of the other ways in which women's lives are interpolated by issues of class, race or sexuality.

A key difficulty of organising in dancing (and in the sex industry more broadly) is that spokepersons for dancers are consistently dismissed as 'inauthentic', a key mechanism used to silence workers in their attempts to speak and be heard. As we show in Chapter 4, there is no such thing as 'real' or 'authentic' dancer (or rather there is no such thing as an 'unreal' or 'inauthentic' dancers), due to the heterogeneity of the social characteristics of dancers and their reasons for selling their labour in the strip industry. Just as there is no such thing as the 'prostitute' because of the heterogeneous nature of experience (Chapkis 1997), nor is there any such thing as the 'dancer'. Eliding differences between women (based on class, race or sexuality) and between clubs (in terms of autonomy and management practices), by making gender the single most powerful axis of oppression silences workers in the erotic dance industry from talking about the exploitation they face. Such generalisation also disguises the intensely variable working conditions, standards and experiences within the erotic dance industry and the sex industry more broadly.

Asserting that stripping work constitutes work, as it represents an exchange of labour for money-capital, is not to assert any normative judgement about its value or quality. It is not to assert that it is a 'positive career choice for women' (Jeffreys 2008; Women's Support Project, no date) (though it does not deny this either), but simply that it is a form of waged labour.[2] The routine silencing of sex workers through such discursive means, as well as through claims of false consciousness or 'in-authenticity' is a theft, not only of personhood but also of the grounds from which to launch collective struggles for self-determination. To identify dancers as

Dancers interviewed

Alexandra, 29, Russian. She had originally come to work in the UK as a chambermaid, having paid an agent to find the work. Finding that she was being paid extremely poor wages in high intensity working conditions, she got into dancing through an agent, who she paid £100 for the connection. Through her dancing over the last five years, she bought a house and now lives in an extremely expensive part of London with her partner. She now only dances occasionally.

Anna, 27, white British. She started dancing at 21 to fund her way through a university course in fashion photography. She currently dances in one of the strip pubs, but is hoping to leave fairly soon. She likes the dancing partly because she enjoys doing pole dancing and pole shows.

Bella, 26, white British. She started dancing at 22 to fund a degree in make-up artistry (having already got one degree). She has danced in a number of clubs, but currently dances at a large chain and lives with a number of other dancers in London. She plans to stay in the industry for a few more years and then wants to pay for her training as a yoga teacher and eventually leave. She likes her job and uses it mainly to have freedom in her life to travel and have a flexible lifestyle.

Chiara, 22, white British. A full-time sociology undergraduate student, she is single with no children. She lives in a large northern town and combines dancing with a job in fashion retail. She has been dancing for just over a year and she dances because she likes 'nice things'. She has worked in two clubs and works two or three times a week.

Dalia, 20, white British. She started dancing when she was 18 and has been dancing for two years. Working in a large northern town, she is not a student and hopes to open a pole dancing studio with her friend.

Eerikka, 36, Finnish. Following redundancy from television work, she found herself stuck. With a friend dancing at the age of 32, she started dancing and is now a postgraduate student undertaking a master's degree.

Emma, 31, Belgian. She is highly educated and extremely articulate, with a degree from Oxford. She has worked in numerous jobs from television to councils and

local government, but has always returned to dancing. She has worked in dancing for thirteen years and enjoys working in the clubs in London.

Edie, 33, white British. She has worked in clubs for over a decade in the UK and
is also a musician and performer. She has been quite involved activism against
the introduction of nil policies.

Faith, 34, white British. She has been involved in a lot of union activity around
dancing. She started dancing because she felt a vocation towards it. She has
been dancing for eight years.

Gabriela, 32, Spanish/Venezuelan. As she has a European parent, she has the
right to work in Europe. She is a dancer in other types of shows and in circus-
type acts at festivals and other events. Having left Venezuela in 1997, she plans
to move to the Canary Islands soon. She has a partner who also works in the
indirect sector of the sex industry.

Heidi, 26, white British. She is from a home county and lives with her partner.
She is undertaking training in beauty and sports massage and first started off
dancing in shows, but has worked in a number of clubs as well. She has been
dancing for five years.

Ines, 35, Spanish. She started dancing in Miami while on holiday and working
as an air hostess, before returning to work in London. She now has a daytime
job working in property and letting management, but still dances every now
and then. She has danced in many places across London as well as in Europe
through an agency. She has been dancing for over ten years.

Julia, 25, white British. Having done pole dancing classes as a leisure and fitness
activity two years before, she started dancing on her twenty-second birthday,
after her placement year in law. When she returned to complete her third year,
she did not want to lose the income that she had become accustomed to. Now
25, she has a stable £30,000 a year job working for a public contractor. She said
she worked to finish paying off debts, to be able to go on an expensive holiday
and for the kick of earning a lot of cash and taking it home.

Katy, 25, white British. She started dancing at 18, using the income to fund travelling in the United States and Australia. She is in between jobs, but just applied
for a job as a life model.

Kasia, 23, Polish. Kasia came to the UK on her own, five years ago, knowing
nobody. She first went to work as a nanny for a family in the home counties.
She was paid £80 a week and did not have a good experience. She stayed in that
job for five months and then did other jobs such as factory work and packing
for two years. She finally found work in a strip club and has been doing this
for three years.

Kristina, 25, Estonian. She has been dancing for two years and intends to return
home after six months or so. She found out about the work from a friend who
came to England, so she decided to try it for a short time.

Lana, 23, white British. She works in a club in the north of England, having started dancing two and a half years ago. She previously worked in admin and sales out of school, but she much prefers this job, as it is more fun and now also does glamour and commercial modelling.

Laura, 28, white British. She is an ex-dancer who is now working as a solicitor. As a student, her house mates all had bar jobs where they earned about £20 a night for long hours. Keen to do well on her law degree course, she decided against taking a bar job as a student, choosing instead to do podium dancing every few weekends from age 18. Having trained as a gymnast when she was younger, she found pole work very easy. She recently stopped dancing to focus on her law career.

Maria, 31, Italian. She has a partner, but lives on her own, and studies Astrology and mediumship in her spare time. She has worked in around ten clubs for the past few years and currently works in a strip pub.

Matilda, 24, white British. She is dancing full time 'at the moment' and has been dancing for around two years. She first started dancing part-time while studying at university and started working after this, moving in and out of the industry ever since. She now works full-time in a club in a north-east location.

Nina, 26, white British. She started dancing four or five years ago. She is single, has no children and lives in a large northern city. She has worked at all the clubs in that city and some in other large cities and is in full-time undergraduate education. Before she started dancing she was a recruitment consultant. She has since worked in about ten clubs, travelling around the country working in different places.

Olive, 21, white British. She started dancing a year ago and lives at home with her parents, studying speech therapy in her home university.

Poppy, 21, mixed heritage British. She started dancing three years ago and lives with a flatmate in the city. She dances in a different city to the one that she lives, in the north of England. This is her main job but she is considering going to college to do her A-levels.

Rebekah, 25, white British. She has no children, is single, and holds an NVQ but is planning to take up science-related undergraduate study. Hairdressing has been her current job for four and a half years in the north of England and abroad in Australia. She started dancing when she ran out of money whilst travelling in Sydney. As she had lost her hairdressing clients when she returned, she looked for stripping work whilst she decided what her next path was.

Stefania, 39, Romanian. She is self-educated to a high level. She works sporadically, coming for a few months or a year at a time and returns home where she works as a sex therapist. She specialises in sex education and is trying to get the Romanian government to change their policy on sex education.

Sophie, 31, white US American. She dances in the strip pubs and has danced there for over a decade. She likes dancing and it is her main job.

Sarah, 34, white British. She was introduced to dancing by a close friend. After they returned from travelling, they were in need of work in London and went to one of the largest establishments to try it. After earning £400 on her first night she was hooked and has worked (often solely dancing) for nearly twelve years and in most of the establishments in London. Through a Canadian dancing agency she has also travelled and worked in dancing in many worldwide destinations including Japan (pasty bars), Puerto Rico and Australia.

Suzanna, 38, white British, began independent dancing as a form of feminist protest when she was rejected by commercial strip clubs and was raising two children on her own. She stopped dancing many years ago but has worked in the adult industry in various capacities, off and on, for ten years, and is committed to campaigning for change and greater respect as part of her work as a thinker.

Una, 29, Estonia. She has been in the UK for six years and has excellent English. She has a child back in Estonia and an Estonian boyfriend in the UK. She has worked as a dancer for two years and sends money back to her family to look after her child.

Vida, 26, white British. She has been dancing on and off for five years and is a highly articulate and intelligent graduate. She is now moving cities and using dancing to help her while she looks for other long term work.

Index